In 1972 James was our number one works F3 driver. When the car didn't work very well at Monaco, he told the world it was no good, which was probably true. I took the view that this was not what a works driver should do and after a discussion we sacked him.

Max Mosley, President of the FIA

He was one of the ultimate characters of the era.

Mario Andretti, driver

He was an absolutely marvellous father. This was not the public persona at all.

Professor Sid Watkins, Formula 1 medical supremo

He was building a very competitive stud and he didn't want to exploit his celebrity. In budgie circles he wanted to be known as a decent breeder and exhibitor.

Mick Mapston, budgerigar breeder

We didn't really go out very much, our house was our castle. We took the dogs out quite a lot on the common and went cycling but really normal stuff – going to the supermarket.

Helen Dyson, fiancée

Other books by this author:

GRAND PRIX CENTURY
The first 100 years of the world's
most glamorous and dangerous sport

MEMORIES OF AYRTON

INSIDE THE MIND OF THE GRAND PRIX DRIVER
The psychology of the fastest men on earth:
sex, danger and everything else

JUAN PABLO MONTOYA

THE MOTORSPORT ART OF JUAN CARLOS FERRIGNO

MICHAEL SCHUMACHER
The greatest of all

AYRTON SENNA
The whole story

AYRTON SENNA
As time goes by

MURRAY WALKER
The very last word

HITLER'S GRANDS PRIX IN ENGLAND
Donington 1937 and 1938

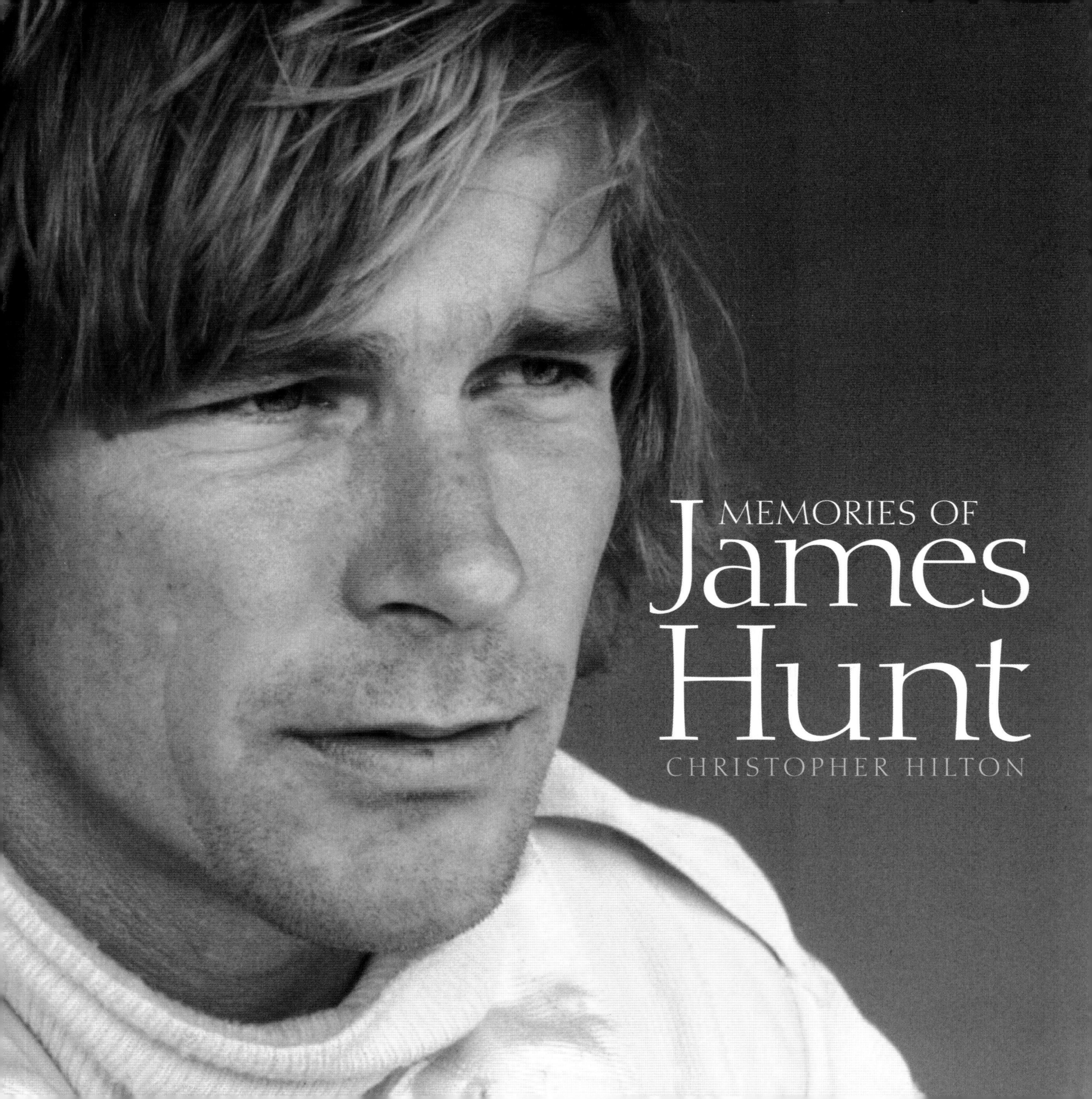
MEMORIES OF
James
Hunt
CHRISTOPHER HILTON

First published in April 2006

A catalogue record for this book is available from the British Library

ISBN 1 84425 215 9

Library of Congress catalog card no 2005935258

Published by Haynes Publishing, Sparkford, Yeovil, Somerset BA22 7JJ, UK
Tel: 01963 442030 Fax: 01963 440001
Int.tel: +44 1963 442030 Int.fax: +44 1963 440001
E-mail: sales@haynes.co.uk
Website: www.haynes.co.uk

Haynes North America Inc., 861 Lawrence Drive, Newbury Park, California 91320, USA

Designed and typeset by G&M Designs Limited, Raunds, Northamptonshire
Printed and bound in Britain by J. H. Haynes & Co. Ltd., Sparkford

CONTENTS

INTRODUCTION

If you follow modern Grand Prix racing – whether by reading about it, going to the races or watching them on television – and know little of its history, the life and times of James Simon Wallis Hunt will come as a complete shock.

As I write, this was posted on www.grandprix.com/ns/ns14145.html: 'In November, Räikkönen was photographed on the island of Gran Canaria, obviously rather the worse for drink. He later apologised for his behaviour. One would have thought that this would be the end of the matter and that drivers in the modern era would learn from their mistakes and be a little more discreet about their activities, but last weekend a British newspaper alleged another series of saucy revelations about Kimi getting drunk and wild in a lap-dancing club called For Your Eyes Only in London's swanky Mayfair district.'

James Hunt *was* a lap-dancing club.

He was also a man of bewildering strengths, weaknesses and contradictions – hence this book.

A word of explanation. To mark the tenth anniversary of Ayrton Senna's death Haynes published *Memories of Ayrton,* constructed around a simple question to those who knew him: what is your strongest memory? They could answer whatever they wanted, they did and it suddenly opened up unexpected – and unexplored – avenues to Senna's many facets.

It demanded a successor but who to do next?

Most modern racing drivers are cast in one dimension and most other people are too. They simply don't have the facets to explore – but, in direct contrast to the whole lot of them, James Hunt contained within himself a whole exotic array. You will see the moment you get into his lap-dancing club.

He was quite different from Senna in every important sense – except that they both drove and had a tangible, almost Hollywood-kissed charisma – and, as a consequence, this collection of memories moves in different directions, assumes a different feel. One example among many. Hunt ended his life so hard up that he rode a ladies bicycle to get around, Senna ended his life constructing a business empire ...

I thank the many people who broached the memories for their honesty, even when it was clearly uncomfortable for them. They insisted, with an almost haunting unanimity, that whatever their feelings about him and his sometimes outrageous conduct, the truth needed to be told – not least because that's what he did himself, and that's the way he would have preferred it.

There's no need to name the people broaching the memories because in each case that's in the text. I've given their occupations as they were at the time.

For illustrations, thanks to Martin Hadwen of the Motor Racing Archive, Hugh Maclennan, Juan-Carlos Ferrigno (via Christine Mills of Planners International) and particularly Helen Dyson for lending a heartbreakingly touching love letter as well as a superb example of her work as an artist. Donald Taylor, the editor of *Cage and Aviary Birds,* opened their files so that we could reproduce some precious cuttings of another of Hunt's facets, breeding budgerigars.

For help, thanks to the staff of *Niewe Revue,* Amsterdam – who allowed me to raid their precious cuttings – and Wampe de Veer of Sutton Publishing who translated crucial parts of the *Niewe Revue* feature article on the seduction of James.

In his maturity, the face became hewn as it assumed a great dignity (David Hayhoe).

AKE COUR

PART ONE

YOUNG WARRIOR

As a philosopher once remarked, 'we can understand each other, but we can interpret ourselves to ourselves alone.' When considering the contradictory phenomenon that was James Hunt, it's useful to hold those words in mind, because even understanding him proved elusive, never mind interpreting his actions. The memories in this first mosaic have been selected to reflect the affectionate exasperation he often generated. Not all of the anecdotes make comfortable reading but, as such, they are certainly authentic to the man. In his life Hunt, the product of a deeply traditional upbringing, outraged many motorsport insiders by flouting convention. He had done that from the very beginning of his career and that behaviour developed as his fame grew. Bigwigs gasped; fans rejoiced. In the midst of the storm stood a lean, lanky, well-spoken, dishevelled, bohemian Englishman who had decided, consciously or otherwise, that his interpretation of himself was that he was OK just as he was: no need to worry too much about etiquette. If people found him insufferable, it wasn't his problem. But then, having acted the autocrat he might surprise you with kindness. Predictable he wasn't.

***Hunt drove at least ten times at Brands Hatch in Formula 3 in 1969, winning twice. This is after the Courage Kent Messenger race* (LAT Photographic).**

MAN OF MYSTERY

The memories in this opening mosaic have been selected to give a sense of James Hunt. They are mostly self-explanatory, but Nick Brittan encountered Hunt in the most junior category of all, Formula Ford.

NICK BRITTAN

Long-time motorsport activist

James behaved badly throughout his career but managed to turn it into an asset rather than a deficit. I don't know how he did that, because at the time nobody else was behaving badly. If James had been a yob nobody would have paid any heed to him and he'd have been sacked instantly but, because he was your archetypal British public schoolboy, behaving badly was a jolly jape.

It falls into exactly the same category as this: if you are coming home at four o'clock in the morning and there's a drunk lying in the gutter and he's wearing rough clothing and he's unshaven, you think *how revolting*. If ten yards later there's a gentleman in evening dress lying drunk in the same gutter you think *what a splendid evening he must have had*.

That's what James was doing.

So when he was raving and ranting, he wasn't doing that to create an impression: that was James. From the very first moment he was an arrogant public schoolboy at a time when, certainly in Formula Ford, it was honest working lads or young chaps having a go – but nobody who had been to Wellington College. So James was a cut above the average in terms of his background and his education.

The picture that defines a life. Everything Hunt had done before led to this – the championship decider, Mount Fuji, 1976. Everything he did after reflected it (Getty Images).

He got away with it because he was the only one of them, and he was good looking and he was charming, and he had style. He could do something, come back, apologise and look ever so humble – all of that – because it's part of the educational system. If you make a prick of yourself you go to the host and say *I'm terribly, terribly sorry for last night*. What can you do but forgive him?

There'll be more about Brittan's exploits with Master James, culminating in a posh reception in London after the World Championship and a very expressive gesture indeed.

SARAH LOMAX

Second wife

Did James have a short fuse? No. Never. I've read that he was quite lively on the racetrack, got out and decked someone. That's why his home life and other self, let's say, was very, very calm. Very relaxed and nothing like the character he needed to adopt as a racing man. James did not have a short fuse at all. He used to amaze me because he could let things go. Someone would do a wind-up remark, I'd be going mad and he'd have forgotten it. I'd be carrying it for a week and he'd go 'why?' You always admire people who have demanding jobs and the minute they get home they are a family man and nothing like the character they were in the meeting or whatever three hours before. It's only men who take control of their lives who can do that.

Maybe it came across as arrogance that he had, but deep down it wasn't arrogance. There was no arrogance in James as I knew him. It was just his manner or reactions. Stubbornness? Yes. Arrogance? No. In there [gestures to inside] he was very humble in there. Very.

James stayed remarkably grounded despite living in public. Watching other people and reading how they react to constant publicity, it's the most un-grounding thing to be reading about those things all the time. Maybe he was lucky or maybe it was this belief in himself that allowed him to stay grounded. He didn't really lose his head over any of it, did he? Being controversial – that's fine. And if he hadn't been we wouldn't be sitting here having lunch [in November 2005] would we?

JOHN WEBB

Owner, Brands Hatch

I was never close to him and really he caused us nothing but embarrassment. His general behaviour, outside of being a very good racing driver, was quite embarrassing.

RICHARD WEST

Formula 1 sponsorship executive

He was a charming, charming man and I think it's important that this comes across. For all the stories of derring-do and late nights and everything else, there are a lot of stories about James which show him to be an incredibly compassionate human being

I started at McLaren in 1984. He regarded McLaren as his spiritual home and he was very, very close to John Hogan [Marlboro executive]. He and Hogie and Graham Bogle [also of Marlboro] were all really good mates. You can talk about his odd ways and the odd crazy night but he was a fiercely intelligent man. He was very engaging. I remember his fortieth birthday party when they lived in Wimbledon and it was just outrageous. It was a time when Joan Collins was going out with Bill Wiggins, known as Bungalow Bill.[1] They were there, Paddy McNally and Ron and Lisa [Dennis]. It was a fantastic event, a remarkable party and I'd never seen anything like it. He was a great raconteur, great fun, but there was a serious side and when you tapped into that you found an immensely knowledgeable man. And talented. When he did *Superstars* back in the 1970s he blitzed all the top athletes and won it twice.[2]

As a commentator he only didn't show once, at Spa. It makes me laugh thinking back to some of it – I don't think anybody ever truly found out what he did the night before that Belgian Grand Prix.

At the end, when he'd gone through all his other periods – and I don't know why he went through them – he decided it was time to start leading a proper life.

That was why it was so tragic when he was taken the way he was.

There'll be more about his friends, his commentaries and the diametrically opposed views here expressed by Webb and West.

MARIO ANDRETTI

Formula 1 driver

He was one of the ultimate characters of the era, that's for sure.

Were you aware of the English class system?

As such?

He was the product of the English public school system, which are in fact private schools ...

Ah!

So he had a very good education, which in theory gave him a privileged position in life.

It seemed indeed – and I don't think there was any question – he was intelligent or well educated, well spoken. He was certainly a man of the world. I think James had all those attributes but he was also the ultimate free spirit. I personally like to see that in a person. I'm not sure I agree with everything, like going to a gala event barefooted, things like that. It takes a certain individual to be able to do that and pretty much get away with it. But it seemed like he always wanted to make that statement – that he could do whatever he wanted. I think it is like when I look at women. Certain women can have a foul-mouthed swear and get away with it and others, when they do this, it's totally awkward. So with him it seemed like *well, it's James, you know* and you leave it at that. You figure out that's him.

He had the attributes of an absolute superstar, no question. It was so much fun to be around him, especially on the social side, and he could be as good as anyone on any given day on the racetrack, so you had to respect him. He had raw, absolute talent.

Sneak preview of the seduction of Hunt: see The Seductress *in the chapter* SOUND AND FURY *(courtesy* Nieuwe Revue*).*

„Ik ben verlegen. Vooral voor groepen mensen. Ik houd niet van volle ruimtes. Het laatste jaar is dat erger geworden, omdat iedereen nu naar me kijkt."

foto's: Willie van Klink e.a.

JAMES AAIT HEERLIJK

Nieuwe Revu's troetelreporter ging naar Spanje om coureur James Hunt te interviewen. Onmiddellijk raakte ze in de ban van z'n blonde lokken en donkere wimpers. En de wereldkampioen formule I bewees meteen dat hij niet alleen op de weg een flitsendsnelle jongen is.

32

„Maar wat mijn vriendin betreft, ben ik nu soms een beetje jaloers. Als ik denk wat ze allemaal doet in New York... maar ik weet wat ze doet, dus eigenlijk is het geen probleem."

We rijden naar de haven in een vierpersoons Seat en niet in de Porsche die ook voor de deur staat. Hunt houdt er niet meer van op te vallen door zijn auto.

„Je rok staat mooi bij je benen, zegt hij. „Heel sexy." Een beetje verbaasd vraag ik me af of hij zich tijdens het rennen soms zou hebben voorgenomen me dit compliment te maken.

Just James. In 1980 motorists could buy stamps to help save for their vehicle licence. Hunt nose it makes sense and helps with the publicity (Getty Images).

IAN PHILLIPS

Journalist

My strongest memory of him is principally intelligence. He always worked everything out so that he did the least amount possible to achieve his objective in the smallest amount of time possible. On top of that, he had enormous fun doing it! In his Formula 2 days we were driving from the Nürburgring to Pau, which is at the foot of the Pyrenees, but we had time for a couple of days holiday – rest and relaxation – in Barcelona. We were driving the Hesketh Racing Grenada estate and in the boot he set up a stereo system. The trick was to drive as quickly but as tidily as possible so that the needle didn't jump off the LP record, which was playing the 'Trumpet Voluntary'! He didn't regard this as unusual, it was just to keep us amused on this rather tedious journey – but we only had the 'Trumpet Voluntary'.

GERALD DONALDSON

Hunt biographer

Everybody who knew him well liked him. A lot of people who didn't know him well hated him but they saw aspects of his character which were not the full picture – actually, nobody hated him, that's too strong a word. He was disliked by some people.

He was a very decent fellow. He straightened out all his problems in the last couple of years of his life, stopped drinking, chasing women, became fit and fell in love for the first time – which I think was the catalyst.

There was a lot of emotion spent in the production of that book[3] by a lot of people because they felt strongly about him. A lot of tears were spilled on the manuscript. My tears too? I don't know about that, but it was quite a shock when he died because I was close to him for several years. We were doing his newspaper columns and so on. In fact that's how we got together.

I had never actually talked to the guy. This was, I guess, 1989 or 1990, in the Silverstone parking lot. He came striding towards me and pointed his finger at me.

Hunt: 'Donaldson, you bastard. You had me in tears.'

(Donaldson: *what the hell have I done?*)

Hunt: 'I've just finished your Villeneuve book.[4] Well, what's your next project?'

Donaldson: 'How about the *James Hunt Memoirs?*'

Hunt: 'No, not time for that but let's get together.'

So he was kind about my Villeneuve book and I started working on his newspaper columns. It was a *lot* of work because he was extremely painstaking about it, dotting all the i's, crossing all the t's, changing terminology. We worked very, very hard on his columns. Some people sort of thought he 'fluffed' off his work but I know very differently.

Smoothly does it on the way to Barcelona (cartoon by Julian Kirk).

KIRK
TRUMPET VOLUNTARY

He talked about being in the public eye and how difficult it was to keep your head in such a heady environment. He was surrounded by interesting characters – characters tend to attract characters, and he certainly did.

SIMON TAYLOR

BBC radio commentator

His dressing up in an irreverent way for formal occasions was exactly like a public schoolboy who wants to put two fingers up to the authorities, and if he's told to wear a tie he will immediately stop wearing a tie – but at the same time he wants to captain the first XV, get into university and get on with the goals that he has set himself.

There's also a very well known public school *thing*, which is not uncommon, where you desperately want to do well but you let everybody know that you don't care, so that if you fail people will think *well actually he wasn't trying very hard anyway.* It's a dotty English middle class thing, not so much now but in the 1950s and 1960s, a defence mechanism, while in fact underneath you're trying bloody hard. So it may have been that.

What stays with me is that James was a clever bloke. He thought about motor racing very hard in a way that not very many other drivers did. I remember sitting with him in the McLaren motorhome once and he was saying 'the thing is, it isn't possible to be World Champion in Formula 1 unless you've got a fair bit of intelligence', and just at that moment a certain former champion walked past the window. James said 'mind you, there are exceptions to every rule ...'

CHRIS WITTY

Competitor and Formula1 PR

There were times when he used to wind people up. He'd go into a bar and if there was a pretty girl and an ugly girl he'd always have a bet with the mechanics that he would pull the ugly one – because she didn't expect to be bonked that night and he couldn't be bothered to spend all the time chatting up the pretty one. There's a wonderful story, and I think it goes back

A beautiful study of power by celebrated artist Juan Carlos Ferrigno (courtesy of Planners International).

Marlboro

Just James, roaming the paddock dressed any way he wanted – but at least this time he wasn't barefoot (David Hayhoe).

to when he was racing with McLaren at Watkins Glen, that he did it. That was just wonderful rebelliousness, wasn't it? *I don't have to have the best as long as I get satisfaction*. That was perhaps his view of life, really, in some respects.

PERRY McCARTHY

Driver

When I was a kid coming through, and looking at these guys, there was a little club of them that I thought were just fantastic: Keke Rosberg, James, Niki Lauda, Alan Jones. To me they were men's men who liked a pint, liked playing up and then would get into a race car and have their balls round their neck – that fast. And that's the kind of thing I have always looked up to. I would never criticise the boys who are technocrats, looking at computer printouts at four in the morning, I seriously wouldn't, but my club is that little mob. Really, from the outset I think that I had a soft spot for James and those of that ilk.

JOHN WATSON

Driver

I think it *was* a part of him, even if only indirectly, and the Press did contribute to this because the amount of Media attention he was getting was not that of a racing driver – it was disproportionate. James was delighted when Suzy [his first wife] ran off with Richard Burton. That was probably more valuable to him than winning the World Championship because it took him off the sports pages and put him onto the news pages.

James acknowledged, and ultimately accepted, that you can go down two routes. You can be a fairly anonymous World Champion, and there have been a number of those, or you can be a World Champion who is prepared to do a Dorian Gray[5] and sell your soul for your looks. James embraced that.

As a consequence, you start to have this *paparazzi* intrusiveness in your life where you can't get out of bed in the morning without someone with a zoom lens looking into your life. That's all fun at the time but eventually it's tiresome and then *very* intrusive. That is part and parcel of that level of fame – like David Beckham. I'd say Beckham is the James Hunt of today. Everywhere

Nearly three decades after Hunt won the world title, his was the image chosen for an invitation to a Formula 1 end-of-season party. This is Brazil 2004 (courtesy Bob Constanduros).

DID SOMEONE SAY PARTY?
LUCKY·TRIBE

Hunt and the A35 Austin van he could make go fast (News Group/Rex Features).

the guy goes he's news, and James was of that magnitude as a sports celebrity.

Having won the World Championship he didn't shrink, he went the other way and it was something he enjoyed.

Then there was the perversity of his attitude – not just to authority *per se* but in particular what you'd normally describe as manners: turning up at formal functions in a manner which was provocative and offended people. That was an aspect of his nature – *to hell with them, do what you like.* But they needed him more than he needed them, and that's very often the case when you get a particular personality.

I contrast that with when he had children. You could see the love in him for his children and it was lovely to see it. I also contrast that with the role Burt Lancaster played in the film *Birdman of Alcatraz.* James became the birdman of Wimbledon! He had an aviary and he went to budgerigar shows. Suddenly here's a guy who in the 1970s was the playboy of the western world going in the late 1980s and early 1990s to budgie shows in his A35 van and competing for – ironically – 'bird of the competition'. It was the real man coming through. His stage had changed and he was reverting to childhood.

Once upon a time I went to interview The Gorilla of Monza, as Vittorio Brambilla was known. He told me an anecdote about Hunt and, although this has appeared before in F1 Racing magazine, it bears repetition, not least because The Gorilla went to his last resting place in 2001.

VITTORIO BRAMBILLA

Formula 1 driver

I had just one 'discussion' with Hunt, at Hockenheim. Hunt was on the last fast lap for the qualifying and it was the last corner before the pits. I am going slowly with my hand up and it was a problem for Hunt. When we got back to the pits Hunt crashed into my car. We got out and he said 'I don't like this nonsense.' I punched Hunt on the top of the helmet like 'zis' – boom, boom, boom – and that was our discussion. Bernie Ecclestone put a stop to it. He said 'you stop that and I will speak with Hunt.' Hunt was crazy angry.

Notes

1. Joan Collins had an affair with handsome property dealer, 'Bungalow' Bill Wiggins.
2. *Superstars* was a BBC TV programme which pitted famous athletes from different sports against each other, often with surprising results. Although the competition was artificial (ie created for television) the competitive instincts of the sportspeople was evident all the way through.
3. *James Hunt: The Biography* by Gerald Donaldson (Virgin Books, London, 2003).
4. *Gilles Villeneuve: The Life of the Legendary Racing Driver* by Gerald Donaldson (MRP, Croydon, England, 1989).
5. *The Picture of Dorian Gray*, by Oscar Wilde, looks at the link between youthful beauty and morality.

The long, hard road: Formula 3 at Silverstone 1970 and Hunt didn't win, he didn't get in the top three (LAT Photographic).

STROL
27
30

Marlboro

STATELY PORTALS

James Simon Wallis Hunt was born at Sutton, Surrey, on 29 August 1947. At the age of seven he was sent to Westerleigh Preparatory School. His other brothers – Peter, Timothy and David – would all go there too.

The headmaster, James Wheeler, remembered Hunt showed talent at sport and, more unexpectedly, a talent for knitting. He'd sit up in bed and knit socks for his little sister Georgina. Of more significance, as Wheeler attested, was the fact that Hunt was in no sense embarrassed doing this.

Wellington College followed in natural progression, as it would for all the sons. There, Hunt excelled at sport, and the Director of Music, Nigel Davison, remembered he gave 'a fine account of the slow movement of Haydn's trumpet concerto while still in the lower school'.

But let's start with Hunt's sister Sally and his second wife, Sarah Lomax, reminiscing these many years later about James and their two sons, Tom and Freddie, and cutting the lawn ...

SARAH LOMAX

The lawn mower? Tom is a stripe man and Freddie crashes it. He has no regard for machinery at all. No interest. James's lawn mower we still have. Tom uses that one, a little green Atco. He does wonderful stripes.

Why did James do stripes?

Ask his elder sister, not me.

SALLY HUNT

He used to mow the lawn a lot when we were little. I don't know if that was his job or Daddy made him do it.

SARAH LOMAX

He'd start again if he made a wiggly stripe. He'd go over and over until it was right. And he always completed a job, whether it was emptying the bins or doing the budgies, whereas I'd probably have five different things going on at once.

The imagery of a lifetime. Hunt, podium, champagne, smiling faces – he's just won the 1976 Race of Champions at Brands Hatch but it could have been many, many other places (Getty Images).

J. R. RICHARDSON

Lifelong friend

I knew him from the age of 12. We lived about a hundred yards apart and so the friendship from childhood was an act of fate – a whole group of us were in the same area of Cheam [in the heart of stockbroker Surrey] and basically we had the same interests, like every teenage group. We played football, rugby, ran, went down to the tennis club and all that. *He* played tennis very, very well and played squash very well, which I didn't do. At Cheam sports club I played hockey and his dad Wallis was a leading light. I didn't go to Wellington, I was at Cranleigh.

TAORMINA RIECK

Girlfriend, known as Ping

We were about 13 at the time – I was just a few months younger than him so we were the same vintage – and

Taormina Rieck, nicknamed Ping, and affectionately referred to by James as 'Tom Trich', the teenage girlfriend still drawing delight from those early days (Author).

both members of the local tennis club. That was Sutton hard courts. He was a very good tennis player and an exceedingly good squash player. He had a friend called Dennis but one day the two of them had a huge argument – huge, huge argument. We were playing doubles. I can't remember who Dennis was playing with. We went on court and they wouldn't say a word to each other. It was the funniest match you've ever come across. I can't remember who won – well, whoever was the crosser of the two of them probably lost.

James had a great big aviary in the back garden and he was mad keen on the things – budgies – when he was a teenager. He had a parrot called Humbert.

Peter, the brother, had a party and we go-karted round their house in Cheam but James wasn't there.

Virtually every ambitious youngster starts like that but James wasn't interested.

RICHARD LLOYD

Old Wellingtonian

The Wellington motto is *heroum filii* – Sons of Heroes. It was a military school and meant to feed people to Sandhurst [the British Army's famous officer training academy]. It was a traditional public school at the top end, then of course entirely male dominated. Now it's got girlies all around the place and it's not quite what it was. From memory it was quite big, 700 pupils. There is no history of motor racing other than [Williams designer] Patrick Head who went there.

TAORMINA RIECK

I remember going to a ball at Wellington. He took me along to go with one of his friends. James and I started off as being just great friends, we played tennis together and we didn't start going out together until we were – oh, I can't remember, probably about 17. He was dressed as he should have been at the ball, DJ.

When I was about 18 I went to the RAC Club in Pall Mall because he was playing in the national championships. I went along to watch. I got to the door and they said 'no ladies allowed'. I said 'oh, come off it' and James being James said 'oh, don't be so stupid, of course you've got to have ladies watching.' So I was secreted in, and the most stupid thing was that all the doors of the men's changing rooms were wide open and they took me down past them!

He was the sort of squash player who ran and ran. All his matches went on for ages. He was so fit and I think he was the first racing driver who really brought fitness into the equation.

HUGH MACLENNAN

Wellington contemporary

He lived differently from most of us. He was good but dangerous company. I was just a few months older than him and we were classmates. He was bright but he was irritating because he'd always disrupt the class. When you actually wanted to learn something James was in the way!

He could have been a professional squash player, tennis player, athletics, ski-ing, golf.

I ended up being captain of the cross country running team. He was on the team. We'd have a race about every other Saturday against another school. He would not show up for our training runs, he would smoke and, when the races came, it was as if he was in a different league. He would win the damned things! That was determination.

Wellington was an old-fashioned English public school – and think of the time we were there. I started there in 1960, James started in 1961 and he left in 1967 when he started racing. It was very traditional, and of course it was a one-sex school, which was a problem for James.

He played the trumpet quite well, actually.

Wellington was a disadvantage because some kids were rich but many were not, including myself. Looking back, it was appalling the sacrifices our parents made to send you to those schools. At Wellington, frankly, if you were very bright they paid attention to you and you could go to Oxbridge or Sandhurst, but if you weren't doing either of those two things then *bugger you!* There were 60 teachers at Wellington and every single one of them had gone to Oxbridge except one who had gone to some 'unknown' university like London. One master had actually worked in industry – I think for only six months – so he was the careers master because he knew about all that.

At Wellington I became, in my senior year, the president of the motor club. I put a lot of effort into that. I got Denis Jenkinson to come and speak. Richard Shepherd Baron[1] with Chris Lawrence came in seventh at Le Mans [in 1962] in a Morgan. Anyway, Baron brought the bloody Morgan along and the driveway at Wellington was a straight kilometre. We got him to do a standing start kilometre. James never showed up to any of this because he wasn't interested.

There was a clubman's meeting at Silverstone in 1966 and the brother of Hunt's doubles tennis partner was in one of the races. Hunt watched and was intoxicated. More than that, he worked out that these were ordinary people going racing with what they could save. He was going to do it.

HUGH MACLENNAN

Then all of a sudden, just as we were about to leave the school – saying *oh my God, what are we going to do?* – James comes up to me and says: 'well, you know a bit about cars, Hugh, how do I become a professional racing driver?' So here's an 18-year-old saying *I am going to become a professional racing driver.* You think *oh, yeah, right.*

TAORMINA RIECK

I remember going to Brands Hatch with him, right at the beginning when he first started watching racing, and it was the Boxing Day meeting. We were sitting there and he just came to life. 'Isn't it wonderful? I've got to be involved in this. This is for me.'

He worked. He did porters' jobs, he did all sorts of menial jobs. I think an idea was for him to go into the Army, and he'd probably have been very good there, but the motor racing came along. He was terribly sick before races, even in the Mini racing days. He had these nerves right from the word go.

He won a Grovewood Award[2] and we had to buy a suit specially, because he was told he wouldn't get the prize unless he went dressed properly. I remember going and buying this damn thing. I don't remember ever seeing him wear it again.

He always called me Tom Trich – don't know why, it was his own particular name for me. My maiden name was Rich.

Who was James? He ... if something interested him he went for it 100%, as he did with most of his sport. Even when he did his job, when he worked for Telephone Rentals to raise money, he did that 100%. Actually he had to dress properly there too I should think. He could talk the hind legs off a donkey, charm people. His parents, I suppose quite rightly, weren't going to have anything to do with providing him with cash for motor racing.

Who was James? He was ... he was a very good friend, right to the end. We remained great friends. Basically, his life took on another direction, he always had an eye for the girls and I said 'enough's enough.' In fact, at Monaco at the Grand Prix I met my husband to be – 1970.

J. R. RICHARDSON

We were holiday mates and I didn't really start meeting him regularly until he was about 15. I think his interest in women lent a bit to our relationship as well. He discovered women extremely early – and once he'd discovered them he didn't forget!

What was he like as a teenager? Always very single minded, very affable, as I say, very keen on ladies – you know, when you're growing into it, as one does. He was very good-looking, very non-standard – what's the word I'm trying to find? – unorthodox.

Bohemian?

That would be fair enough. A very unusual man but very well liked, very sociable but very single-minded. He was his own guy without compromise and that's a good description, a *very* single-minded chap.

The family intention was for him to go to medical school. But he had a driving licence and he'd discovered driving fast.

The Cheam 'team' of friends used to drive down to East Grinstead and race back. He crashed his car on a couple of occasions! Listen, you're 17 and you're driving all these weird cars as far as you can from East Grinstead and Chris Jones was in his MGB ... yes, Jones – not James! James had a Mini for a while, then one time he had his father's new car which I think was a Fiat. He'd only had it for about a week and that got badly dented. Someone else was sent in to explain to dad that it had been a terrible accident but was not James's fault. Wallis of course showed his normal disdain: 'you're still not getting any bloody money.'

TAORMINA RIECK

And of course all the cars of his mother that he wrote off. He was notorious for that. The Hunt household, because there were six children, was a very easy, friendly atmosphere. One was always welcome and I still talk to Pete and I bumped into Dave a few months ago. They're all characters in their own right.

J. R. RICHARDSON

He played great golf but years later when he'd retired he tried to re-model his swing and it simply didn't work. He had difficulty with his rounded shoulders, which made his swing look funny. He was shooting high 70s and mid 70s, and if you go to the club down at Woodcote Park you'll see his name on the board for their knock out championship. I think he shot high 70s to win that competition, playing off about 26!

That was due to Wellington, really, where he was much better at the individual sports than he was at the team sports. I'm not sure that he represented Wellington at anything except tennis, squash and cross country running.

He had a charisma all his life which wasn't dependent on the World Championship he won. He had charisma *and* the World Championship. He had it in those early days. He was a very popular figure, a sportsman, very good looking and he had the sort of focus, I always thought, that led him to become the World Champion. Even at that age it was extremely apparent, albeit not focused on motor racing until he went to his first motor race.

CHRIS MARSHALL

Team owner and friend

I liked him enormously. I respected his intelligence, if you like. He had been offered a place at medical school and he would, I think, have made a brilliant doctor but he made a very quick decision, having been to a couple of club races, that he was just hooked on racing. He was single minded about it and he drove his parents crazy – James had an elder sister who became a barrister, and of course his parents were firm believers in education. They sent all their sons to Wellington which, as the old boy [Wallis] said, kept him honest – Wellington fees multiplied by four.

BRIAN JONES

Brands Hatch commentator

I know the stories that abound when James went through the driving school at Brands. The truth is that although he spent quite a lot of money and went all the way through the course, in those days the acid test of whether or not you were going to make it as a racing driver was what they called the Class 2 Test. That consisted of driving in the reverse direction around the short circuit, what's now called the Indy circuit.

If you go the wrong way round, the circuit becomes effectively entirely different. You are new to it and you have to demonstrate the ability to come to terms with it. For example, travelling the reverse direction down Brabham Straight into Clearways is really quite daunting because you have to hang on to the power a lot longer than you expect.

The instructor would go out in a Formula Ford, or whatever they were running then, and set a representative time rather than going balls out for a good time. That would be the measuring stick.

After the instructor had set the time the pupils went out and did three laps familiarisation, came in, then had five laps to get to within, I think, half a second of the representative time. On two occasions James failed the Class 2 Test. Eventually he stormed off and he never had a good thing to say about racing schools.

In a way I understand why, because everybody thought a racing school was a licence to print money, but in fact it wasn't anything like that. It was damned hard work.

HUGH MACLENNAN

I can't remember if James and I actually went together to the racing drivers' school or if it was on separate occasions. Here's the deal and I owe James a lot. When I found out what he had done compared to what I had done, and that he was obviously so superior to me, right there I said *well, I'm never going to be able to earn a living by racing*. And I never tried.

JOHN WEBB

In those days the racing school were tenants of ours – we didn't run it as we later did – so I didn't know he'd done

The Wellington cross country team, Hunt seated front left, with Hugh Maclennan next to him (courtesy Hugh Maclennan).

it. I do remember him as one of the first competitors in Formula Ford in 1968, which I started. I also remember he was sponsored by a company called Vincent's of Reading, who were Rolls-Royce agents. As a train spotter during the war I'd pressed my nose against their showroom window outside Reading station to have a look at the Rolls-Royces. So when he appeared, driving for Vincent's of Reading, it revived memories. He was a very competitive driver in Formula Ford and he went on from there to Formula 3, where he was also competitive.

Hunt bought a Mini shell and spent almost two years building this, took it to Snetterton circuit in Norfolk for his debut – and failed scrutineering because it had no windscreen. To have a public schoolboy in motor racing provoked plenty of comment. He raced a time or two in 1967.

J. R. RICHARDSON

He took the Mini apart on one occasion ... in order that it became compliant with the regulations. That was typical James, in a way, and he did it all himself. That was another thing which was widely admired: he saved everything. I remember when he cut down to three cigarettes a day so that he could save the money for the other seven out of a pack of ten. It was very serious and most people don't behave like that.

TONY DRON

Driver

James Hunt was undeniably a product of the public school system, and of Wellington in particular, yet the persistent image of a wealthy young playboy could not be further from the truth. In 1968, James was on £20 a week, working (I think as a salesman) for Telephone Rentals. To get started in racing he had two hire purchase deals, one on a new Russell-Alexis Formula Ford car and another on a specially prepared engine. He was well into his F3 career, with the Russell-Alexis long since written off, before he paid these off. His tow-car in 1968 was an ancient, rusty, pre-Farina[5] Austin Cambridge saloon worth less than £60. We dossed down in places like the press box at Snetterton to avoid paying B&B prices.

It's all very well being brought up in those nice houses (James came from Belmont, my parents lived in North Drive, Wentworth Estate – they were similar places), being sent to expensive schools and enjoying that comfortable start in life, but if you turn your back on convention, avoiding a 'sensible career', and there's no money available, life does become a serious struggle straight away. We were committed to race driving, not playing with it. The objective was to get to the very top.

TAORMINA RIECK

At the start we all helped. There was the classic occasion with the famed Mini when the trailer gave up the ghost. We were coming back from Silverstone. The police came and said we'd have to leave it parked on the side of the road.

Hunt: 'I'm not leaving my car there. By the time I get back it'll have vanished. Bits will have gone from it. I have to tow it home.'

Police: 'Yes, sir, but you're not allowed to tow on the motorway.'

Yet again he used his persuasive charm and had this frayed old bit of rope. I sat in the Mini, which had no windows, and it was a winter's evening, pitch dark. I was towed down the M1, through London and out the other side to Cheam. When we got there he said 'well done, Tom Trich. There's two threads of the rope left and you've made it without breaking it.' We all did it because we wanted him to succeed.

There was a determination about the man. He had it with his squash. He was so determined to win those matches that he would not give up. He just carried on running and running and he would wear the opposition down.

I remember talking to Keith Wooldridge, who was a very good tennis player [and became Women's National Training Manager]. James played him a few times and Keith said it was an absolute nightmare. One always knew the match would go on and on and on. I think James played for the county, so he was an extremely good standard.

HUGH MACLENNAN

I can remember going to races in the very early days with him where, right before he was going to get in the car, he disappeared. He was vomiting behind some trailer. He was so focused and so determined that it was amazing. I do remember going to his house on many occasions because we lived fairly close by. I can remember him running with Wallis, his dad. His dad looked very young and his dad must have been very fit so it was passed on, in that sense.

I remember in 1967 at Brands Hatch talking to him as he was going to the grid. He had decided to take the plunge and buy a Formula Ford [for 1968]. He got into bed with Gowring's of Reading, the big Ford dealer who sponsored him. He called me up and said 'Hugh, I need a tow car. Can you help?' A friend of mine owned a garage down in Sussex and he bought this A95 – that was a big ugly Austin. We bought it for nothing – five quid, ten quid – and that was the tow car. One of the reasons the A95 was so cheap was that it was burning oil so, whenever we drained the Formula Ford engine oil, we poured it into the A95 to get home. He had a trailer and we'd load the Formula Ford on to that.

His very first helmet he gave to me – I needed a new one. Typical James: *you take this one.* Graham Hill put the London Rowing Club's colours on his helmet and James put the Wellington colours on his. Did I think he was going to make it? What a great question! No! But he would not let anything stand in his way. My mother used to say 'God, he's hard.' I do remember going to some garage in northwest London. His sister was there and the subject came up about gaskets and he thought cornflake packets were just as good. If you used them you could save a buck or two.

In 1968 Hunt drove in ten Formula Ford races, winning the second of them at Lydden Hill. Oulton Park was the sixth round.

ANDY MARRIOTT

Journalist

Part of what a school like Wellington does is give somebody self-confidence. James was able to get away with a lot because of that, but it's a double-edged thing. He probably had the confidence but then he also had the tag of being a public schoolboy. That didn't fit very well, certainly in those days – it's probably easier now. But the school probably did knock him into shape.

CHRIS WITTY

The public schoolboy? Well, you could go back to the 1930s, 1940s and 1950s and they were all like that. He

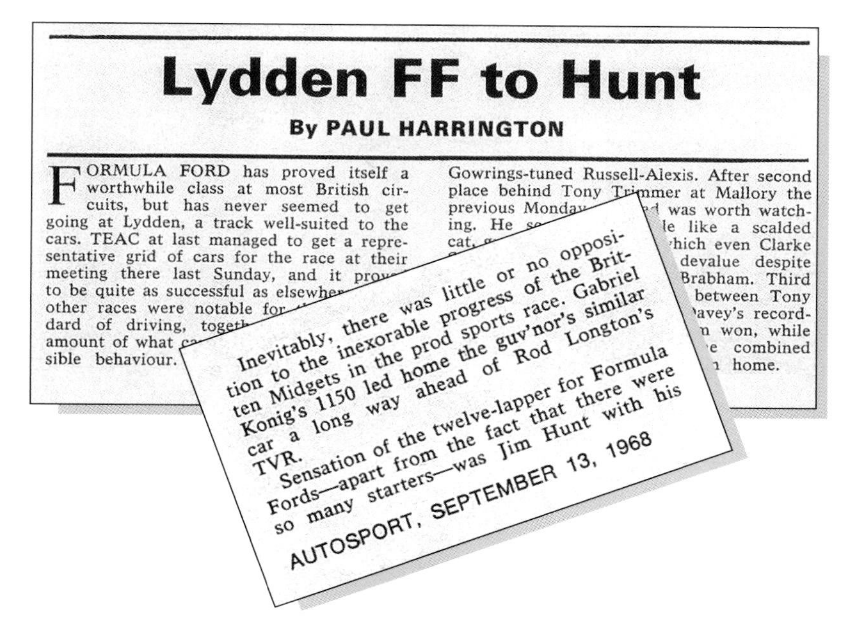

Lydden FF to Hunt

By PAUL HARRINGTON

FORMULA FORD has proved itself a worthwhile class at most British circuits, but has never seemed to get going at Lydden, a track well-suited to the cars. TEAC at last managed to get a representative grid of cars for the race at their meeting there last Sunday, and it prov... to be quite as successful as elsewher... other races were notable for... dard of driving, togeth... amount of what ca... sible behaviour.

Gowrings-tuned Russell-Alexis. After second place behind Tony Trimmer at Mallory the previous Monda... was worth watching. He ... le like a scalded cat, ... which even Clarke ... devalue despite ... Brabham. Third ... between Tony ... Davey's record... won, while ... combined ... home.

Inevitably, there was little or no opposition to the inexorable progress of the British Midgets in the prod sports race. Gabriel Konig's 1150 led home the guv'nor's similar car a long way ahead of Rod Longton's TVR.

Sensation of the twelve-lapper for Formula Fords—apart from the fact that there were so many starters—was Jim Hunt with his

AUTOSPORT, SEPTEMBER 13, 1968

A life in headlines, starting small – and as Jim! – Hunt gets a write-up in his first full motorsport season, 1968 (Autosport).

was of the old school in that respect. Maybe if he'd been born today it might have been a lot harder for him. It's all timing. I don't know whether he would have conformed in the way that they are forced to conform today and lose their personalities.

I must have met him in 1968 when he had just started Formula Ford. I was doing the *Motoring News* reports at Brands Hatch and he was in the winter Formula Ford series. He had a Merlyn[5] with Gowring's as his sponsor. He was doing it at the same time as Tony Dron, Tony Trimmer, those people. Formula Ford is really how you get to know all these guys. I never actually thought he'd make it in the early days because there was nothing other than guts and determination, no magic, no spark that forced you to think *the guy is going to be a World Champion.* In a way he did do it through guts and determination.

In those early days he was driving round in a little Mini and he was a big guy. He didn't drive the Mini when he had his Formula Ford because it wouldn't tow it but he had something fairly dated, the racing car on an open trailer, that sort of thing. He didn't turn up saying *look at me, I'm rich* – and anyway he wasn't! But he was rich in his mind because he came from the moneyed background.

I remember going to where the family lived. His brother David was only about six or seven. Mum and dad were very upper middle class and professional people. You felt that they'd got the boys, they were going through public school and that was the way they were. I didn't see a lot of – how can I put it? – tactile love there in that respect. It was the way that families were brought up and that's not a criticism, just the way it was.

TAORMINA RIECK

I remember the time that James went through the hoarding at Oulton Park in Formula Ford! In those good old days I was in the pits doing lap charts and keeping times with a stopwatch. Great fun. He particularly liked it because, rather than doing the numbers of the cars, I did the initials of the people and so when he came in he'd look at it and say 'oh, right, I overtook so and so.'

Everyone in Formula Ford knew everyone. He sailed off through this hoarding and into the lake. They hauled him out and he was really quite shocked. The Dron drove the two of us home, I seem to remember. James went into the water and got wet and was not at all pleased. He wasn't that good a swimmer ...

He was happy in the beginning, yes. I think probably because he had to work so hard to get where he did, he really appreciated it when he got there. When he got the first drive for March the joy was *I've done it all myself.* His

sweaters had great holes in the arms. His shoes had holes in them and he was always complaining 'my feet are cold because it's wet outside.' There was no money to resole the shoes. And he drove in a really ancient old pre-war Rover [the Austin came next] which didn't start quite often, and one would have to push the damned thing, this huge great lump of a car.

NICK BRITTAN

I ran a programme called Formula Ford International. I'd been very much involved in 1968 in the creation of Formula Ford and a spin-off was called Formula Ford International. My brief from the Ford Motor Company was to introduce Formula Ford to the six 'Ford' European countries: Sweden, Belgium, France, Germany, Switzerland and Italy. They were called the ESO countries, whatever that meant. In order to do this I used to package up races of 20 cars and put them into existing race meetings in those six countries. For example, when there was a Formula 2 race in Belgium at Zolder I'd package up a race of English drivers and put them on the grid at that meeting in order to introduce Formula Ford to Belgium. And so on.

It was a very good deal for the race organisers because they got a very exciting motor race happening on their

Hunt's second race abroad: a 1969 Formula Ford race at Aspern, an aerodrome near Vienna, where he missed all the bales and finished second (LAT Photographic).

circuit which was totally pre-packaged for them. It was like ordering from a catalogue. *What sort of race would you like, Monsieur? I can give you cars of the following colours, all of which are driven by young Brits, all of whom are fearless, many of whom are guaranteed to spin off. It will be* très *exciting! And there will only be a small charge.*

Over a period of 18 months I did 34 races all over those places and it was good fun. These young guys in Formula Ford were desperately keen to do it because it meant they could go international.

'Where did you race last weekend? Brands Hatch, Castle Combe?'

'Oh no, I was at Zolder in Belgium.'

'Well, I was at Hockenheim in Germany.'

'Oh well, you're an international star.'

Fantastic! The race organisers used to buy the package from me, I used to give the guys 20 quid start money and they'd work it out for themselves. It also made the Ford Motor Company smile because what happened as this went on was that it became popular in Belgium and the next time the Belgian organisers wanted a race they would order only 15 cars because by now there were five Belgians, who owned cars. Eventually I went out of business by design.

This must have been 1969 and I was living in Islington at the time. One morning there was a knock on my door and there was a little guy, all of 5ft nothing, and a big guy. The big guy had a *big* head of hair and a pockmarked face. The little guy, called Chico, spoke English. He said 'my name is Chico, I am from Brazil and you are Formula Ford and I want to introduce you to Mr. Fittipaldi. He doesn't speak English but he wants to race in Formula Ford. Can you 'elp us?' I said 'come in ...'

They did come in and Emerson sat there grinning while Chico spoke.

You had to pay five quid to be a member of Formula Ford International so Chico gave me five quid.

At the same time there was a very arrogant young English chap – public schoolboy called James Hunt. James was getting a deal together to come into Formula Ford. The bottom line was that, a matter of months afterwards I put one of my events together to go to Vallelunga in Italy, and amongst the lads were E. Fittipaldi Esq. and J. Hunt Esq. Not a bad double for a tenner!

So I took 20 guys down to Vallelunga. In those days everybody had to have a certificate saying what your blood group was, a meaningless thing but that was part of the deal. When you signed on with the organisers, they knew that allegedly that was your blood group. So who had turned up without a certificate? J. Hunt Esq. So J. Hunt. Esq. was ranting and raving with the organisers. I listened to this for a while and then went over to him. I said 'James, go to the local hospital now.' It was eleven o'clock on the Saturday morning. 'Hurry to the local hospital, get them to give you a blood test.' But he carried on ranting and raving, telling the organisers this was bloody stupid. I tapped him on the shoulder and said [sotto voce] 'come over here. James, if you are trying to be a professional racing driver and you carry on like this, you won't make it as long as you have got a hole in your arse. Now get up to the ******* hospital and do what I tell you.' 'Oh, all right.'

James did a few more races with me, learned to behave himself and eventually graduated out of Formula Ford into Formula 3, and onwards and upwards.

In April Hunt was due to drive at Aspern, a track on an aerodrome near Vienna (see picture on previous spread). Beyond motorsport, fidelity was a perennial problem for Hunt.

TAORMINA RIECK

Gerry Birrell[4] was one of the Formula 3 drivers who James raced against and the first time I met Gerry was in Austria. I drove over – James was already out there and Gerry and James became good pals because John Hogan took them both on and tried to get sponsorship for them. I became great friends with Gerry's wife. Now the first time I met him was a few weeks before he was getting married and Gerry often said 'I can't understand how anyone can behave like that.' Quite often I would hear from Gerry and Margaret, 'God, he's been off again.' It was nothing personal – he did it, I think, to all the women in his life, didn't he?

SIMON TAYLOR

Funnily enough his career – in terms of years – paralleled my journalistic career. I first knew James when he was driving in Formula Ford. There were a couple of people called Mike [Tisehurst] and Gerard, two rather wild public schoolboys. Gerard I knew because he lived in a mews house just round the corner from me in Kensington. Gerard had a bit of money and Mike was a bit of a wheeler-dealer. They started a company called Motor Racing Enterprises, rather grandly. They were trying to become a racing car dealership in a way that they reckoned hadn't been done before, and in the midst of all of this they stumbled over James who, like them, was a slightly rah-rah public schoolboy. James ended up in a Formula Ford car and had large accidents and wins in roughly equal proportion.

ANDY MARRIOTT

I knew him from when he was in Formula Ford. I was around the scene – we were similar ages and so on. Obviously he had to deliver on the racetrack and that's what he did. All those good looks, all that charisma, all that Wellington College education wouldn't have mattered a jot if the guy couldn't drive. In fact it could have been a hindrance. He was a Hooray Henry who *could* drive! In Formula Ford he was Hunt the Shunt, fast and dangerous. But you know he was honing a talent, and successfully honing a talent. James managed to get some money together – I think Coca Cola put some in.

His career went in stages, didn't it? First the Formula Ford stuff with those two guys who ran his Formula Ford car – Mike Tisehurst and the other one. They were very important to him and I believe they funded a lot of that. They were public school mates, I think.

I launched the March Formula 3 car – Ronnie Peterson was the driver of that, but he got injured and James took over.

Taormina Rieck was called after the town in Sicily because that's where she was conceived. He called her Ping. She was the first girlfriend and the sort of girlfriend you expected him to have. She was a stunning woman, very, very bright and she steered his career to a degree.

JOHN WEBB

He won a Grovewood Award in 1969. At that time it was about the best thing you could win and ironically years later he found himself presenting Grovewood Awards to other people – and not many have done that.

The intensity of a racing life, written into his face (LAT Photographic).

Notes

1. In fact they were thirteenth overall but first in their class.
2. The Grovewood Awards, extremely prestigious and a way of recognising young talent. The 1969 Awards went to a Formula 5000 driver (first), Hunt of Formula 3 (second) and a Formula Ford driver (third). It suggested, as much as these things ever can, a big future: the 1970s might be his decade.
3. A delightful way of saying the car was old. Giuseppe Farina won the first World Championship in 1950 ...
4. Gerry Birrell was a driver with much promise, killed in a Formula 2 race in 1973.

THE SHUNT

In 1970 Hunt drove a full season of Formula 3 in a Lotus 59, starting at Silverstone in April and then moving to Magny-Cours a week later.

TAORMINA RIECK

James was already in France and I drove down with Margaret Birrell and Gerry's sponsor. We arrived fairly late in the evening so we'd had a long day's travelling and James was nowhere to be seen. Typical James. Lord knows where he was. This chap said 'would you come and share my room?' 'No thank you!'

James did then appear and I was absolutely furious but we had a good couple of day's racing and fun [Hunt finished fourth]. We went out to dinner on the last night, all the Formula 3 chaps – it was the days when all the English got together and went out, had good fun. The steak that I asked for was totally inedible and I sent it back. It was probably horsemeat. Then they brought me another one and that was even worse, like leather. I said 'I can't eat that.' When the bill came I refused to pay.

They called the police and it ended up with James, a journalist and myself being taken off in a police van. We got to the police station and James said 'come on, Tom Trich, blub.' So I did and we talked them round – 'this is ridiculous, we'd have paid if we'd eaten it.' In the end the police took us back to our hotel. They felt desperately sorry for us. This was typical James: he wasn't going to let them get away with it.

We then decided that we were going to go straight to Monaco. He'd got a blue light that he put on the roof of the car. If we came across any blockages on the way we'd put this flashing blue light on and went straight through.

Then we were driving to Austria but he didn't have the right paperwork, so James, the mechanic and myself had to drive to the smallest, least likely customs point to get through. I think we rocked up there just before it was closing at some ungodly hour of the night. We were waved through – and the relief! He was determined to get there to race.

We had the most wonderful time at the Österreichring because March were there testing with Jo [Seppe] Siffert. Jo had got out of the car and was lying on the pit wall while the team were fiddling around with the car. Robin Herd said to James and myself 'I want to go and see how the car behaves on a certain corner. D'you want to come? Get in the [hire] car and we'll go round and have a look.'

We got in the car and Seppe was still lying prone on the wall. He must have been up and into his [Grand Prix] car in a matter of seconds because we were going up the hill and round the first corner and Seppe buzzed us. He went past us on the right-hand side. Robin Herd was talking away to James and suddenly ... we all nearly died. Herd said 'I'll get the bugger, I'll get him.' It was such a shock – this F1 car coming past us! Can you imagine that happening today? It wouldn't be allowed – certainly not one of the bosses being given the fright of his life.

James loved it and that sort of thing all made it worthwhile for him.

By August Hunt had driven 12 times, won at Rouen, been second three times and third three times. The next two races were in Sweden.

HUGH MACLENNAN

James called and said 'would you like to go to Scandinavia with me as my companion?' I said 'yes, sure.' So I end up in the passenger seat of this Ford Transit van with the mechanic driving. I felt so sorry for him. We were towing

Moving up. This is the Hesketh March 712 at Brands Hatch in the 1972 Rothmans 50,000 series. Hunt finished fifth in a very strong field (LAT Photographic).

the Lotus 59. In the back of the Transit van was, amongst other things, a 50-gallon drum of gasoline. I said 'James, why the hell are we shipping gasoline to Scandinavia?' He said 'oh well, I was given it.' He answered my question like *what a stupid question to ask*. I don't know how we got through customs!

For some reason James overtook us in his MGB GT on the hard shoulder, he didn't do it where everybody else overtook us – on the road.

When we get to Karlskoga, James introduced me to a bloke called Andy Sutcliffe. He was what I could have been – a guy who thought he was going to make a living out of motor racing but actually didn't have the ability. Then James says to me in the next breath 'Andy's mechanic has quit. Would you like to stand in for him?' so I thought *yeah, sure*. What James didn't tell me was that every time Andy went out the bloody thing crashed: I had just enrolled myself for a 24-hour a day job. Sure enough, Andy goes out – he was also in a Lotus – and knocks a corner off it and breaks an upright. There was a guy in the paddock, a very nice engineer for a Swedish gun manufacturer who had a factory nearby. He opened up the factory for me and proceeded to weld this upright.

Andy and James had enticed a lady to go out to dinner with us. James decides to give her a driving lesson in her Volkswagen on a twisty, gravelly mountain road. James was in the passenger seat giving her instructions. I'm following in Andy's Volkswagen transporter. Of course the poor lady obviously lost her nerve, overcooked it and rolled the car. Fortunately no-one's hurt. We put the car back on its four wheels. This girl – nice girl – was the daughter of the guy who was doing all the catering for this race meeting.

The next morning we roll up and she rolls up in her VW with a dented roof. The father comes up and we're all sprawled over the roof trying to hide all the dents because of course the father owned the car.

To James that was just another weekend.

The key to that season was that you could make a living – just – in Formula 3 if you managed your expenses. You got start money, so you had to start and that's why I was having to work like a beaver on Andy's car.

The second last race of the season, at Crystal Palace, culminated in Hunt and Dave Morgan crashing, Hunt springing out of his wrecked Lotus and thumping Morgan. It became notorious, not least because the race was televised.

ANDY MARRIOTT

Crystal Palace? James wore his colours on his sleeve. He was what he was. There was no side to him. He was outspoken: God knows what he'd make of motor racing today. He'd probably be outraged.

I don't think he was a natural but he had set his heart on being an international race driver, he overcame some of his limitations and just went for it. That's the measure of the man. He was treating it as a personal crusade. If he'd gone into the Army he'd have probably made a brilliant brigadier or something by hard work.

I didn't find it easy to talk to him. He was very impatient, he just wanted to get on to the next thing and long conversations weren't really appealing to him. He was a driven guy. He started actually quite late. Nowadays they come out of these junior formulae and they're surrounded by managers. James was the last of the true, swashbuckling, British Formula 1 drivers.

In 1971 Hunt contested Formula 3 again, now driving a March 713. He crashed heavily at Zandvoort, Holland, the eighth race. Monaco was a week later.

TAORMINA RIECK

He couldn't help it [womanising]. It's as he was. I could see a look in his eye when he was denying it all. You just knew and he knew you knew. Stories would come back. I was still seeing James and he said 'right, you are coming down to Monaco again this year' and I said 'no, I'm not, James. That's it. I want to be friends, I don't want to fall out but I'm not being treated like this any more. I'd rather remain friends than fall out.' I think he found it a little hard to take.

CHRIS MARSHALL

Running F3 team

I'd met James in 1970. I had started the 1971 season with a driver who'd won a Grovewood Award but unfortunately he didn't turn out to be as quick as we'd

Driving lessons in Sweden (cartoon by Julian Kirk).

KIRK

hoped. James had started the season running his own team with a loaned chassis from March but he'd had his umpteenth crash at Zandvoort – he ended up at Tarzan horseshoe upside down. He'd gone from Zandvoort down to Monaco and he arrived with plaster all over his nose, his hand bandaged because he'd ripped all the skin off. He hung around our pit. After the race I was sitting on the back of our transporter going up the hill under the shadow of the castle. It was a really hot day and the traffic was slow. He was walking along the pavement and he saw me. He hooked himself up on to the tailgate and we chatted.

Hunt: 'I'm glad I've found you because I am going to drive for you.'

Marshall: 'Well, I've got a driver.'

Hunt: 'Don't worry about that. Your car is always immaculate, it's always first out to practise and it always finishes. You do that for me and I'll win the championship.'

So by the time we got back to London – he had a lift with me – we did a deal. I sold a chassis and Max Mosley gave me another one for James on the strength of that. Then I got a friend of mine, Chris Andrews, to sponsor it and off we went with the March works team for the second half of the season.

He really got his nickname [Hunt the Shunt] driving for me, I think. Of 31 races, including heats, we won ten and crashed in eleven. It really was win or bust and that's the trouble with single-seaters. If you come together and the wheels interlock, somebody's going to go up in the air. Sometimes it was the other guy, sometimes it was James but you had to get that close. You tried to hit wheel-to-wheel but you couldn't always do it.

He took all that very philosophically, *just one of those things*.

In 1971 we had restrictors on the air intake and the cars weren't tremendously powerful. As a result, the skill of planning your race was in slipstreaming [getting a 'tow' from other cars, then nipping out and overtaking them]. That was where James was so brilliant. Afterwards he would sit down in the truck and we'd go through the race. He could recall every lap and all the manoeuvres and who did what. I used to write it down. I've had a lot of drivers and very, very few could do that.

That was really useful, and James would learn. During a race he'd try one side and the guy would move over; or he'd dive down the inside and see how he got on; and whatever happened he'd remember it. During a race he'd rehearse the last lap or two – whenever he was going to make the big effort – so he'd know what the bloke was going to do. But of course if the other guy wanted to be on the same piece of concrete – bingo.

On several occasions he'd be sick before he got in the car. In fact there were times when he got out of the car on the grid and went and was ill over the barrier. I think it was a combination of adrenaline and the build up of tension. It was a necessary release for him. I don't think he was necessarily terrified, it wasn't fear, it was tension – more of a physical state.

Before the race, in an attempt to calm him, we would often walk around the paddock arm in arm and rehearse the first lap. If he was on the front row I'd say 'OK, now you're in first gear, moving off, second, now third, now you're coming in to the first corner. If so-and-so is alongside you, what are you going to do?' Or 'if you're in front who do you do' or 'if he's in front' same thing. We'd do that for each corner round the first lap and we'd got it clear in his mind – and the main thing was that his mind was off the *hurting* aspect. I'd get him back, sit him in the car and my job was to keep everybody away from him, adoring females, whatever, *get out of the way*. I've got a photo of him sitting in the car staring into the distance and he couldn't see anybody around him because he was concentrating so much.

NIKI LAUDA

Driver

I first met him in 1971 when I came to England to drive for the semi-works March F2 team. I really didn't know too many people and rented a studio flat from Max Mosley at the back of Victoria Station. It was through that connection with March that I really got to know James. He lived in Fulham, as I recall, and despite the fact that we were pretty direct rivals we knocked around a lot together and became good friends.[1]

LORD HESKETH

Team owner

Look at what James did in the 713 March compared to the works Marches. It was no contest.

Personal scrapbook of the trip to Scandinavia in 1970 and Formula 3 races at Karlskoga and Knutsdorp (courtesy Hugh Maclennan).

JAMES' FORD VAN + F3 LOTUS IN SWEDEN.
ANDY SUTCLIFFE AND HIS VW TRANSPORTER
HUGH – THE VIEW FROM THE VW DRIVING NON-STOP BACK TO HETHEL
ANDY SUTCLIFFE
JAMES' IN SWEDEN – THE MECHANIC
Shell
Daily Mail
FORMULA FORD.
The famous A95 AUSTIN WESTMINSTER tow car that I found, whose excessive oil consumption was supplemented after every race with the used oil from the FF.

The 1972 season proved shambolic and complicated. Amidst all that, Hunt found his future. He drove Formula 3 for March until Monaco when they delivered him a car he felt wasn't raceworthy.

MAX MOSLEY

Co-founder March Engineering

In 1972 James was our No.1 works F3 driver. When the car didn't work very well at Monaco, he told the world it was no good, which was probably true. I took the view that this was not what a works driver should do and after a discussion we sacked him.

So he drove for Marshall's La Vie Claire team there and at the next race, Chimay in Belgium, partnering Jean-Pierre Jarier.

JEAN-PIERRE JARIER

Driver

You know, I got along very well with him because we were all the time together in London at night in the restaurants and nightclubs. He liked women, of course, yes, like most of the people at that time in motor racing! He liked them in big numbers because he was ready to go with girls not so beautiful, huh?

I remember a girl I saw in a garage one day in the south of London – it was a small garage – and the girl, she was really awful, really *awful*, and she told me she went out with him. I couldn't believe that because at that time he was already famous, he was *somebody* in England and everywhere. I saw beautiful girls with him and also I saw ugly girls. That's life, huh?

Going into a bar to pick up an ugly girl? It's not my theory!

One day he went after my briefcase. I came out of a restaurant and he nearly hit me with the car. The briefcase fell down and he went with his car on my briefcase. I don't know why! I was not happy at all, huh? But he was drunk that night.

Another time we were testing at Goodwood and he lost the car in the south corner, went upside down and he had the anti-roll bar into the earth. I came, I tried to get him out of the car and it didn't catch fire. Because he had had many shunts in the days before, I said to him 'you're not James Hunt, you're James Shunt.' And he was not happy with me but, you know, he had broken my briefcase the week before ...

He was a brave man, he was strong, he was fearless, he was the guy walking into the party at night with no shoes and no socks, but he was a real fighter so I admired him, yes. He had no limits. He drank too much, he started with a few drugs – Niki Lauda told me that, but I knew – and he had no limits, no limits with Bubbles Horsley and all the gang! Unfortunately he paid a big price for that with the heart.

He couldn't stop. At a certain time in his life he had money, he had fame, and he was unable to save his health. He was a good guy.

At Chimay everything changed.

MAX MOSLEY

So as not to destroy his career, we lent him a 1971 F2 chassis without an engine and he managed to persuade Hesketh to provide him with an engine. I think this was the beginning of his racing relationship with Hesketh. He then went F2 racing as a privateer and at Oulton Park – I think – was in front of the 1972 cars driven by Ronnie Peterson and Niki Lauda. Like the F3 cars, the 1972 version was inferior to the 1971 version. James's performance at Oulton Park rather proved his point about the F3 car.

LORD HESKETH

Why did I start a racing team? Ah ... that's a very good question ... I think mainly by accident. I think the guilty party is Bubbles. He had raced in the 1960s and they rented a line of lock-ups in the Goldhawk Road – Frank Williams, Charles Lucas, Jochen Rindt, Piers Courage, Charlie Creighton-Stewart, the usual crowd.[2] They all trundled round Europe with three sets of tyres on the back.

Anyway, Bubbles thought he'd like to have a go at Formula 3 again. I didn't know anything about racing except that they used to come and stay with me to go to Silverstone, because it was handy. I was very keen on cars and making mechanical things so that's how I got in.

The plan was we were going to run a not very expensive car, built for us by a guy called Geoff Rumble. It was the Dastle Mark 9, which was put together in a barn, funnily enough near to Ken Tyrrell's yard. It was very clean and all sealed in polythene. The weather was hot and the heat was unbelievable because there was no ventilation. Anyway, we went to the first meeting, Thruxton, and Bubbles came past the pits very fast but seemed to drop a lot of time all the way round the back, the reason being that he was keen to demonstrate to his patron that he was trying very hard but avoiding scaring himself too badly on the other three quarters of the circuit I couldn't see.

I didn't know Hunt at this stage, I had no idea at all. We went to Monaco where [young driver] Steve Thompson qualified the car, which we thought was a tremendous success – we'd actually qualified and the fact that we'd got in the race was all that really mattered. Then we went up to Chimay in Belgium, which was a very, very fast circuit in those days. A big circuit too. Triangular, and it was run by some charming Belgian baron – he was promoter, chief marshal, and he had an E-type Jag with no windscreen. The circuit only had three corners, one at the top and one at each corner at the bottom, bit of straw bales, and very fast. There was an army surplus tent, which was all the paddock buildings under one roof.

Preparing for practice in the Formula 3 Lotus 59 at Brands Hatch, October 1970, last race of the season. He finished second (LAT Photographic).

I got there and Bubbles said 'I have hired a driver and become team manager', and I was introduced to James Hunt. Bubbles had found him. He was known to be quick but had a reputation for crashing, hence Hunt the Shunt.

BUBBLES HORSLEY

Team manager

I first met James in 1971. I had stopped driving at the end of 1966. I came back in and that was a mistake. James was very different, he wasn't your typical up-and-coming racing driver of that time, you know. He was quite tricky and argumentative.

When we got together he had fallen out big-time with March and was basically out of a job or about to become out of a job. Although we drove together as a team for the rest of that season the Dastle wasn't very competitive, but everywhere he was a second and a half, two seconds a lap quicker than me. That really told it all.

Hunt made his Hesketh debut in the race after Chimay.

LORD HESKETH

I had great hopes and the first race I watched him drive was at Silverstone. He crashed on the start line coming straight into my feet in the wet, but he improved after that!

GEOFF RUMBLE

Car builder

I used to build oval track cars, not Indianapolis stuff but little cars for running on stock car tracks and that sort of thing. Bubbles Horsley became interested and I built a midget for Bubbles, and Bubbles then decided he wanted an Atlantic.[3] I said I could build him one and he said 'OK.' He thought he might have a sponsor and so we started building this thing. The idea was to do it on a shoestring – well, this wasn't really a shoestring, it was more like a bit of cotton. My midgets were built from breakers' yards. We used to go round the scrap yards to get bits because the Formula 3 car in those days had a tremendous amount of stuff on it that came from ordinary road cars.

After we'd started, Bubbles came up one day and said he'd got somebody who was going to help him with the finance. It turned out to be His Lordship and we built this car, but it got out of hand a bit: they started getting grand ideas about it and they decided, because they wanted to do things a bit grander, they wouldn't do Atlantic, they'd do Formula 3. So I had to change the car into a Formula 3 car.

We had a chap called Steve Thompson – he was quite quick and he drove the car for us at Monaco, the first outing for it with Hesketh. It created a lot of interest, he did very well straight out of the box and we were all very pleased about it.

Then they decided they wanted to do things reasonably seriously. Steve had a lot of business commitments and couldn't accept Hesketh's offer so they looked around for somebody else and James had just had the sack from March. He seemed to be the obvious choice and he had a couple of test drives.

We were going to run two cars: Bubbles in one and Steve in the other. When Steve couldn't take up the commitment James came along. There were a couple of meetings where James and Bubbles drove, but then Bubbles decided that he didn't really want to do it – decided in fact he wasn't really a driver – and then it was just James.

We only had about three or four races and then they decided they wanted to go on to better things – Formula 2. I wasn't really geared up to do that sort of thing and we parted company.

I have to say – it's difficult, isn't it, talking about the deceased? – but I didn't get on with James awfully well. He was quite an ... edgy guy, he more or less chain-smoked. You've heard the stories about him being physically sick before a race. Well, he was very nervy.

I did see him nervous, very much so with the cigarettes – one in each hand. I don't like working with that. Some people can work with that sort of character and I am sure, say, Ken Tyrrell would have done very well because he was the sort of guy who had had all those years of experience of managing people. He'd have calmed him down.

Confirming his potential in 1970: he'd won the Formula 3 round at Rouen and now added Zolder. The Shunt? Out of 18 races that season he had only three accidents and was on the podium 11 times (LAT Photographic).

Mind you, nerves show themselves in different ways. Perhaps he was lucky in that he could show them in an extrovert manner and not build it up. A lot of people – and if I dare mention my own name in such company, because I've done a little bit of club racing – I can get just as nervous as the Grand Prix drivers can who are at a much more exalted level. The way I found it, and I know a lot of Grand Prix drivers do, I used to feel very tired. It was nature's way of coping.

I don't think anybody really took hold of James and tried to manage him – not that he was the sort of guy that you could manage. That wasn't the atmosphere of the Hesketh team, it was *OK, chaps, let's have a jolly good time.*

As a driver he was very fast, obviously, and that's about it. He took a lot of chances, hence all his crashes. I think people thought he was far too flamboyant in style and took too many chances to make it. I personally thought that his psychology wasn't right, the nervousness and the fact that he didn't seem to be able to relax too much.

James was a good looking guy, had long hair, attracted the girls and that's about it really!

BRIAN HENTON

Fellow driver

I can remember when he was crashing Dastle Formula 3 cars with Bubbles Horsley. I raced against him in Formula 3 and he was wild – wild! – then he calmed down because it was the learning process.

This 1972 season Hunt drove seven Formula 2 races, the fifth one at Hockenheim.

BRIAN HART

Engine manufacturer

At Hockenheim Bubbles was trying to keep James in some sort of order. People were apt to show up with girls and Bubbles was trying to keep him away from them – a certain amount, anyway. I remember a picture of Bubbles, a big man, standing with his legs apart and James lying under them looking up at his calf muscles in a very irreverent way.

In 1973 Hunt drove a couple of Formula 2 races in a Surtees car and then Hesketh moved into Formula 1.

JOHN SURTEES

Team owner

He had one of his first drives for Hesketh in one of my cars, a Formula 2, which in fact he crashed. Then he had a drive in a Formula 1 car, which Hesketh got for him and he drove at Brands Hatch [in the Race of Champions, a non-Championship event in March].

TONY DRON

We never raced at Goodwood because that was just before our time, but an awful lot of testing was done there. I heard a funny story about him testing the Surtees there. They're going faster and faster and faster by just trimming off the aerodynamic downforce to the wing. Eventually James said 'well, just take a bit more off' and they said 'you are going to remove *any* downforce.' 'Well, just do it.'

Off he goes, only car on the circuit and – suddenly complete silence. 'Where's he gone?' So everyone's rushing off and eventually they found him over a bank, the Surtees upside down. They were not sure what to do and even thought of knocking on the tub ['anyone at home?']! James emerged and roared 'why the hell didn't you get me out of there quicker!'

BRIAN HART

At Brands Hatch we turned up with an engine, and James and Bubbles had written on the airbox: *Internal Combustion Engine. Nice one Brian!* He drove extremely well and finished third. He did get very heavily motivated, no doubt about that.

What did I make of him as a bloke? Very difficult to answer that. Socially he was a lot of fun. That's all you could say. He enjoyed it – dangerous company.

I think you have to look at it this way: his driving ability peaked a little bit early – in 1976 – and then it went down. He wasn't, for example, like Ayrton Senna who just *knew* how to drive, where to go on which bit of track. Jimbo was forcing himself to do it, and we now know just how much it took out of him physically. He was often sick before a race – but you had the impression that it was all very easy, the public school piece of cake and all the rest of it: the slightly unkempt look about him, for example. He could get away with it and so he was much admired by a lot of people. That made him extraordinarily popular and a magnet for the journalists.

We're coming to all that in just a moment, but before we do ...

TIM CLOWES

Driver insurer

James was a bit of a chameleon: all things to all men. He wasn't the total extrovert that everybody thinks. Whilst he appeared his own man I don't think very many people knew what that man was. Whether it was the drink and the odd snifter off the back of his hand that did it, I don't know. He did quite a lot of that, yes, especially the white stuff. He was burning the candle at all four ends.

I insured him although he wasn't very keen on that sort of thing. It was very much easier to talk to him about his budgies, about which I knew bugger all, than about motor racing. This was very strange. I think that that really pointed out that there was a very private James. I don't think any of the women had a very happy time.

He was not keen on insurance because all racing drivers tend to think they are immortal or they wouldn't actually do it – particularly in those days, when it was dangerous. He was at the end of the era when they did kill themselves with a fair degree of regularity. By the end of his time it was getting pretty damn safe, but when he grew up it wasn't. When I first started doing insurance in 1960 there were about 15 cars on the grid and we never lost less than three drivers a year.

It would be fair to say that at the beginning of his career they weren't really earning an awful lot of money. If you said to them 'if you want a half decent policy it's going to cost you ten grand', in those days that was very serious money.

Even when we were having a drink and a long chat he always tried to be frivolous, possibly because he was frightened or he had a premonition. I don't know.

Not really a tall story. Hunt and Jane Birbeck opened a health club in London and did this for the photographers (Getty Images).

Notes

1. This originally appeared in the magazine *F1 Racing*. I use these extracts with Lauda's permission.
2. Frank Williams, celebrated team owner, of course; Charles Lucas, son of a successful businessman; Jochen Rindt, eventually Formula 1's only posthumous World Champion, 1970; Piers Courage, Formula 1 driver killed in the Dutch Grand Prix, 1970; Charlie Creighton-Stewart, born into wealth, one-time racer and then sponsorship finder.
3. Formula Atlantic, single-seater North American series.

Canon Canon
Canon Canon
Canon Canon

PART TWO

AT WAR WITH HIMSELF

Fame is a heady thing, bestowing constrictions and freedoms at the same time. Big money is more deceptive still, because it promises only freedom. As he moved through his twenties all of this would come to James Hunt in a torrent – a torrent which began with English eccentricity so wonderful that it risked becoming a parody of itself. The torrent flowed urgently to the very serious business of winning the World Championship for a team synonymous with a multi-national company – eccentricity no part of the master plan here – and climaxed one sodden late afternoon beside a mountain on the other side of the world. At that moment Hunt was very famous indeed – at a level of leading film stars and pop singers – and potentially very rich. There was a feeding frenzy around him, in which he sometimes played an enthusiastic part, but that was entirely superficial and he knew it. He was too intelligent to be seduced by such a thing (and we'll be coming to other seductions later in the book). He saw, beyond the autograph hunters and flash bulbs and TV cameras, that his professional career remained what it had always been: very, very dangerous. He wanted to live. Forgive him. He had more to live for than most.

The start at Fuji, 1976. Mario Andretti (Lotus) was on pole, Hunt alongside him (LAT Photographic).

M'LUD AND CHUMS

In 1973 Hesketh did indeed enter Grand Prix racing but, even three decades later, believing it all really happened remains difficult. Here was a Lord with a team nestled into the bosom of his stately home, here was his mother (who wore an eye patch and sold team tee-shirts at Monaco during the Grand Prix), here was Anthony Horsley, and the languid, honey-haired public schoolboy for a driver. Everyone had nicknames, of course: Hunt 'Superstar', Horsley 'Bubbles', the designer Harvey Postlethwaite 'The Doc', Max Mosley 'the great chicken of Bicester', and one journalist 'Superscribe'.

BUBBLES HORSLEY

In a crazy way James and I egged each other on. We weren't very successful in Formula 3, then really showed promise in Formula 2, but actually managed to make a bit of a mess of that. We chose the wrong car for the 1973 season. By the time James had written the Surtees off at Pau we decided *let's go up to Formula 1*. We did everything that you shouldn't do: we failed at Formula 3, we failed at Formula 2, we might as well fail at Formula 1 and then get on with the rest of our lives – but we didn't say that at the time ...

Why run at the back of a Formula 2 grid rather than a Formula 1 grid? That's pretty sensible logic, and there was quite good money in Formula 1. Bernie [Ecclestone] was beginning to get better appearance money, better travel money, better prize money, and of course we were quite quickly running towards the front. By the end of the 1973 F1 season we were threatening to win. In the USA James was almost alongside Ronnie [Peterson] at the finish.

There were two things, really. One: The Doc – Harvey Postlethwaite. He was very good, he knew the car backwards, he was very good at setting the car up and also we got Nigel Stroud and he was very good at preparation. He made the car reliable. He put a lot of little tweaks on and unique things. Two: James was very quick and actually not hard on the car either. Later on,

Lord Hesketh in all his splendour (LAT Photographic).

when we were running Rentaman[1] to help pay the bills in '75, you'd strip down James's car at the end of a Grand Prix and the crown wheel and the pinion would be immaculate, the brakes would be, I won't say untouched but not hammered. Then you'd look at the Rentaman's crown wheel and pinion which would be completely knackered and the brakes would be knackered and that was the difference. James was smooth and quick.

Formula 1 was relatively unsophisticated compared to now. The only way it could be done today is if you were allowed to run customer cars again.[2]

You were widely portrayed in the media as Hooray Henrys because it was almost impossible not to be seduced by Bubbles Horsley, Lord Hesketh, everybody's got nicknames, mum with a patch, the public schoolboy who everybody said should have been a Battle of Britain fighter pilot and somehow people didn't understand that you had a very serious team going on there.

Yeah, yeah, there was. We were actually very, very serious about it but the Leisure Division – the Party Division – run by The Lord got a lot of the column inches. And we did have the strange nicknames. This really wasn't the image of Formula 1 at the time that people like Teddy Mayer at McLaren were trying to portray! I don't think we were universally loved by our fellow competitors, that's a fair thing to say, but James loved it all. It was an environment in which he thrived and I think it was an environment that played a big role in how he matured and became a race winner, then a World Champion. Because we did threaten to win a lot of races: some of them were down to us, quite a few down to him. He could have won the Argentine Grand Prix twice and there were other occasions when we were on for a possible win.

He became a great mate pretty quickly so it wasn't the usual team manager-driver relationship. James was very complicated. There were times when we had patches of non-speaking because he thought I wasn't doing my job properly and I thought he was playing too hard or turning up late, whatever. But he was supremely confident, while quite fragile in that confidence.

He also, I think, suffered from depression which, when he was driving in a Formula 1 car, the whole lifestyle and the fact that your days are completely filled, basically kept it at bay. When he retired, that started to come more into his consciousness and he would have dippers. He suffered from black dog.

He had a slightly addictive personality and he was, you could say, addicted to succeeding. And he was very driven. I mean, he had come through an unbelievably tough journey up to when he met us and it started to go right for him. Many another person would have given up.

He wasn't a rich playboy. He was skint! He didn't have any money at all. He did obviously when he became World Champion, but we didn't pay him very much. I think I settled the outstanding amount – the last payment – I gave him one of The Lord's Porsche Carreras.

None of us made any money out of it. But we weren't in it to make money.

It's a hard question, but do you feel the Hesketh time was almost a deliberate parody of itself?

No, we didn't over-egg it. It was, I think from our point of view, completely natural. We were just ourselves and, where Formula 1 found itself, this was probably the last chance to be that. Three years later it would have been impossible, completely impossible. The last one if you like [to be able to win races] – he didn't party so hard, but hats off to him – was Rob Walker with Stirling [Moss].[5] He was doing better than us on the track but we were doing similar things: private car, no sponsors – the only thing was, in Rob Walker's day I don't think there were any sponsors.

Hunt and Hesketh made their Formula 1 debut in the Race of Champions at Brands Hatch on 18 March 1973 with their March car. It was a non-Championship race and Hunt came third behind Peter Gethin (Chevron) and Denny Hulme (McLaren). Among the non-finishers were Graham Hill (Brabham), Emerson Fittipaldi (Lotus), John Watson (Brabham) and Niki Lauda (BRM).

MAX MOSLEY

At the Race of Champions (I think it was) at Brands Hatch I found Hesketh, James and all their hangers-on sitting in a circle behind the Hesketh transporter. I asked them what was going on and Hesketh said 'We're praying to the great chicken in the sky to bring us an engine, because our only engine has blown up and we're not going to be able to start.' I said 'maybe the great chicken of Bicester could help. I think we can probably lend you an engine.' This then happened and always after that they called me 'great chicken' or, in James' case *'grand poulet'*. I don't quite know why he translated it.

EMERSON FITTIPALDI

Defending World Champion

I'd known James virtually from the beginning although I spoke very little English then. I don't think we raced against each other in Formula Ford because he was in it one year after I did it. In fact, I raced Vallelunga and Chimay in Belgium and Zandvoort in Formula Ford – on the Continent, only those three races. I remember many names that I raced against and I remember those three races very well. My racing was from March 1969 through June, only three to four months. Then in July I started to race in Formula 3, July to October. In 1970 I raced Formula 2 and then in July I was in Formula 1. I think the first time against James was 1970 in Barcelona, Montjuich. I was moving more quickly than he was because in one year and a few months I went from Formula Ford to Formula 1.

Hunt, the athletic all-rounder. When he did 'Superstars' back in the 1970s he beat all the top sportsmen and won the event twice (LAT Photographic).

JAMES HUNT
1

The Hesketh team was very strange. At the end of 1973 Lord Alexander Hesketh invited me to drive for him the year after. I was interested but the team was too new and so I was not sure. I signed with McLaren, and at that time it was a good thing to do.

I knew James and he was always very kind to me, and we had a lot of fun together. I liked to be with James. He was always very nervous before the race. I remember in Formula 1 he always came to my motorhome before the race to get changed – so I had to pay the price of giving James accommodation at most of the Grands Prix!

'Hold on James, don't come in here again.'

'I need it, I need it!'

'OK!'

I don't think Hesketh had a motorhome.

I spent quite a lot of time when he got married with Suzy. She was a great lady and I enjoyed James and Suzy together. Before the Brazilian Grand Prix they used to come down to where I had a house and we'd play tennis, we'd do running on the beach. I had good fun with him. James was always very fit physically, very trim and one of these drivers who surprised everybody when he got to Grand Prix racing.

In Formula 3, in Formula 2, he was never very fast – well, he was fast but not consistent. Then when he got 500 horsepower behind him he went to a better level: he showed more talent with more horsepower and a bigger car. It happens this way for few drivers but James was one of them.

If you look at Grand Prix racing, historically most of the drivers were very good in Formula 3 and Formula 2. Only a few were a big surprise – Niki was the same as James, Niki was never outstanding in Formula 3.

James was very impressive to me as a driver. He had this incredible capacity of being really fast in fast corners. You know, every time I was dicing with him he was always that – and incredible car control, very good with throttle control, natural ability in fast corners. Very committed in fast corners.

ANDY MARRIOTT

James met Bubbles Horsley and Alexander Hesketh and that jumped him forward. Alexander? I don't know. What do you say about him? What they did was great, a fantastic effort, last true independent team – Hunt's victory at Zandvoort [in 1975] was hugely emotional. And it was mega news. James had tremendous confidence in his ability at that time but it was a gung ho approach. *We're all having a jolly jape but we're rather good at this, aren't we?*

Harvey was obviously serious and people around him were too because they put together a serious race car. You can't do that if you're not serious and you don't have a lot of talent.

James came to my flat a number of times and we were involved in judging competitions – motor racing related things. It wasn't to find a new driver or anything like that. I've forgotten the exact details but he took it surprisingly seriously. This was way before he ever got into drugs. I can only tell you that he was in my flat several times and I never saw any sign. He smoked, of course, which I thought was a strange thing for a Grand Prix racing driver to do, but they were cigarettes. I never saw any sign of drugs at all. I think it came later.

He was definitely eccentric. He won something called the Tarmac British Racing Driver and it was at the Grosvenor House. He pitched up with no shoes on and in a tee-shirt at a black tie do, and everyone was looking at him – but he could get away with it, you see. We [CSS] were managing him at the time and we were very cross with him.

You couldn't really discipline somebody like that. You just couldn't. Barrie Gill[4] was very upset because it reflected on us. On the other hand we did a lot of work with Texaco – he and Barrie – and there he was very, very professional. We did a big deal for him once, believe it or not, in Japan with a General Motors brand. He was driving a Ford-powered car [in Formula 1] and we had a deal with Vauxhall. He always carried those out to the letter. He might turn up in some funny gear – there were two sides to James, you see. There was a totally professional public school side – *I have to do the right thing* – but inside there was a rebel fighting to get out, and I think more and more the rebel got out.

You've got to remember that he was probably the last guy to stitch on his race suit something which hadn't been paid for. He had some silly heart with a sexy message ['Sex: The breakfast of champions']. You find any pictures of him in 1976 and you'll see this heart. It was

Suzy Miller, the model who'd become Hunt's first wife, looking at models, and posing like one (LAT Photographic).

something you bought in a shop – an extraordinary thing to do really. He did it just because he wanted to. He thought *that's great, I'm all for that, I'll do it.*

ANN BRADSHAW

Press Relations executive

I remember when they arrived at Brands Hatch with the teddy bears and Alexander and all that sort of thing. It was a lot of fun and I was proud – I had my Hesketh bear tee-shirt but my niece got this and I don't know what happened to it. She wore it until not that long ago. We were proud to do it. It was a time when you were happy to put somebody's tee-shirt on, even though you worked in the sport. You said *great, this is what we are all about.*

DEREK BELL

Racing driver

He was a couple of years behind me as you graduate into Formula 3 and Formula 2 into Formula 1 – then he got ahead of me! I started in 1964 and I was in Formula 1 by 1968–1969. James didn't get there until 1973 so our paths didn't cross that much although he was in events that I

went to. At none of them did I get that close to him. He always had his mob of buddies around him who never let him go because he was such a personality.

Then we went off and did a Dubai Grand Prix and he came on that, as did Niki and everybody else. Even then, when I thought I might get to know him better, I didn't because James was his own man and he did his own thing. He'd walk in with bare feet to meet the Sheik of Arabie, whereas the rest of us were a little more formal or a little more respectful, whichever way you want to put it.

SIMON TAYLOR

I remember the famous crash with David Morgan at Crystal Palace and then I kind of knew James less well when he was at Hesketh because the curious thing about the Hesketh entourage was that you were either a part of it or you weren't. Bubbles almost acted as the bouncer. Alexander didn't terribly want to be bothered with anybody who didn't have a title and several millions. Bubbles filtered the acquaintances and I never got on the inside of that.

The Hesketh team contested their first Grand Prix in 1973 at Monaco (Hunt ninth) and then France (sixth), Britain (fourth), Holland (third).

J. R. RICHARDSON

We used to run together – in the social sense – and then in 1965 I went to Canada until 1973. He was then racing Formula 2 [he did two Formula 2 races before the Monaco debut], and I re-settled back here. He said 'I'm doing this race in Zandvoort' – and that was the first motor race I ever saw. We had a business in Holland. I went to Zandvoort and he got me tickets. This was the race where Roger Williamson was killed[5]. James came third. I watched the race and saw the accident down the back straight, saw the remains of the car and I watched the news with him that evening in his hotel. That was the first time I got a grip on what the real dangers of motor racing were. He was devastated. They knew each other as racers and I think they'd raced each other at junior levels. It was awful for me and I'm sure awful for him because it was so preventable.

July 1974 and the week he became engaged to Suzy he practised the Hesketh at Brands Hatch for the British Grand Prix (Getty Images).

He conquered his fear and got back in – got beyond the physical danger – because of the rewards in terms of his lifestyle and what he could achieve and where he could go. He was always that, in every sport he partook in: golf, tennis, squash. It was his competitiveness, his single-mindedness and his selfishness, I suppose, really. He had World Champion focus in everything, right from the word go.

Incidentally, Hesketh couldn't get sponsorship, which I found astonishing. Anybody with a bit of imagination should have sponsored them.

BUBBLES HORSLEY

It was much more dangerous then. You had Williamson – that was ghastly, that was horrible. That would end up in the courts now.

Austria (retired), Italy (accident in practice), Canada (7), USA (2). In Saturday practice, François Cevert (Tyrrell) crashed fatally.

I would say the 1973 US Grand Prix was the best race James ever drove for us, because he was very aware of the dangers and Cevert had just been killed in a horrendous accident. If you were going to think about that sort of thing, my God it would have got you thinking, and he drove a fantastic race there and it was still his first year and it was in the March against Ronnie [Peterson] and Lotus – and when it was their day they were almost unbeatable. It says a lot that, after Cevert, James was still able to get into the car, but 24 other guys did too. He was sick before races in Formula 1, and being sick was his nervous energy, that was the man in a way. If he wasn't sick before the race we usually didn't get a really good performance out of him. There was no discussion about withdrawing at Watkins Glen, no, none at all.

Hunt finished the season with 14 points, making him eighth in the Championship. Hesketh now built their own car and in it Hunt won the International Trophy at Silverstone early in the season.

LORD HESKETH

You've got to remember that when we won our first race – the *Daily Express* – that was a very bizarre weekend, really. We went up there and the weather was perfect, very unusual because the race was always held in April. We

The wedding at the Brompton Oratory, London. Certain friends wondered if it was more of a team publicity stunt than a love match (Getty Images).

went out, three laps, I think we got round in 1 15.8 – we just shattered the lap record. We brought the car back in and there was nothing else to do. Everyone else was out there struggling and struggling and struggling. Eventually Ronnie got on the front row but he'd done 50 laps or something. Get to the warm up, smashed a front wing hitting a hare but that was OK, switched that over. Then the gearshift lever broke in his hand and he just jammed his palm into the broken top – because there was nothing to push it with. So he then drove a 40-lap race with the top of the gearstick embedded in his hand. And it looked like a mess: he literally crucified his hand to drive the car and to win. He'd dropped 16 places on the first lap. Then he just tore through the field.

CHRIS WITTY

The Doc was fantastic, James would get his head down and there was that tremendous race at Silverstone when he won. Some days he was just electric. In the early days he wasn't a wanker but you just didn't know how long the guy was going to stay around. You'd ask yourself *is he going to do a couple of years and get bored and do something else?* He didn't …

RICHARD LLOYD

Driver, sports car team owner

This is an insight into the psyche of the bloke. James wasn't a very good qualifier. He never quite sorted that out. Apparently Bubbles and the whole team got a bit cheesed off with this because they wanted to get him further up the grid. They noticed that he went better when he was furious and motivated – something had gone wrong – and he'd then go out and do a flying lap. But he wouldn't do it under normal circumstances. So they devised a method: what they did at least once, I know, is that he would come into the pits quite near the end of the session and say 'come on, time to go now, we've only got another four or five minutes' – for his last run. But they'd jack up the back of the car so that he couldn't see what was going on. He knew the car was jacked up and he was getting more and more frustrated, flailing his arms around. Bubbles was saying 'yeah, yeah, we're doing something to the back.' They timed it so that there was just enough for two laps and by the time they'd dropped the car on the ground he was absolutely on the rev limiter. They'd just been messing around doing nothing – but that's how you'd get the best out of him.

BUBBLES HORSLEY

… yes, that is true. He'd be straining away at his seat belts saying 'what's going on?' He'd be waving and gesticulating and you'd see the anger in his eyes. You'd nod to the mechanic, drop the car and say 'it's OK now.' He'd go out and do a blistering lap. And come back and give us a bollocking – 'incompetent amateurs!' One didn't do it every time because it wouldn't work.

DEREK BELL

I drove with him at the Nürburgring in the Mirage in 1974 [in the third round of the World Championship of Makes series]. Well, we were in two Mirages: me with Mike Hailwood, James with Vern Schuppan. Mike and I were running really well, ahead of James, and then suddenly Mike took the car off the road. That was it. I changed into my clothes ready to go home – *I'm out of here*. But of course I'd developed the car and everything, and I was team leader.

John Horton, the team manager, said 'Derek, don't get changed yet, we might need you.' Some time later, in comes James complaining about the steering and said 'I'm not driving that effing thing.' He jumped out of the car and John Horton looked at me and said 'get in.'

Being a dumb-arse I did.

In those days the body all came off from the front and the mechanic is working on the steering. James had had the steering rolling around so I looked at Alan the mechanic and said 'is it going to be all right?' Horton was frantic for me to get out there and I'm looking at Alan – I mean, I've only got to go round 14 miles of track and 160 corners per lap. He said 'yes, it'll be fine.' I always use that analogy when I'm talking about mechanics. I went out and drove faster than anybody had in the car. It was dangerous and you can't expect the team to make him get back in the Mirage but they had me by the short and curlies because I was their number one driver and it was the only drive I really had.

It was interesting because James hadn't got a chance to win. Remember he was from Formula 1 and I was a sports car driver. James thought *I don't want to be tooling round here* – he probably only did it in the first place so he could learn the Nürburgring for the German Grand Prix. *Oh, bollocks, I don't need this* – so any excuse to get out. Drivers in Formula 1 in those days used any excuse to get out, they did. *I got paid my start money, thank God the clutch went.*

Having said that, I think his was a very sensible decision but of course most unlike James, apart from the decision when he quit totally. All the way through, you have to say he was certainly a wild boy.

They called him Hunt the Shunt, didn't they? Now you can't go through shunts if you're an intelligent man and still carry on without working it out. It showed an amazing ability in his brain to say *you're keeping on* when the brain is also saying *this is bloody dangerous*. And it was dangerous, bloody right it was. Look at the blokes that got killed. God almighty. When you think about it, I lost Pedro [Rodriguez] and Jo Siffert in one year – 1971. Of four drivers in the JW Gulf-Porsche team, two got killed and that wasn't unusual.

In 1975, during a difficult season full of retirements, Hunt won the Dutch Grand Prix at Zandvoort. It remains a great feat for such a team, and after it he came second, fourth, retired, second, fifth and fourth, to finish the season on 33 points, fourth in the Championship.

LORD HESKETH

Zandvoort? We knew he was going to do that. We finished fourth in the World Championship that year but we'd had a lousy season because we'd led four Grands Prix by the time we got to Zandvoort. We led in Argentina and finished second: he made a mistake and spun in front of Emerson. We were miles in front at Barcelona when he disregarded the oil flag after the two Ferraris managed to knock themselves out of the race, a particularly fine demonstration of driving. We were leading by a mile in the *Daily Express* International Trophy and blew up.

We should have won Monaco. That was the first time we tried to do what we did at Zandvoort, which was James's theory about the track drying. Therefore you bring the car in far, far sooner and put it on slicks, but we made a mess of the pit stop – and I think if we'd got that right he'd have walked it, and the reason he'd have walked it is that he'd have been gaining time from the minute he went out and everyone would have had to have pitted after him. It was a process of elimination [eliminating the

Le Patron and the employee (LAT Photographic).

others!] and that's what we'd worked out, but of course we hadn't calculated that we'd take 38 or 48 seconds on the pit stop. We just made a mess of it.

Zandvoort had been coming. You've got to remember that in 1975 we were in deep depression – practically on tranquillizers – if we were as bad as the third row. If you average him out on the finishes – all statistics are selective but his achievement in '75 was really quite remarkable. I mean, we should have won Austria. There were only two cars in Austria, Niki and James – it was a two-car race. Unfortunately our Rentaman was so terrified of the wet that he didn't see James behind him and kept holding him up, then that maniac Brambilla closed his eyes and went for it and spun across the finish line.

His finest corner always was Woodcote. He was the only guy who never lifted at Woodcote. They all lifted – Stewart did. Clark didn't and James and Clark are the only two I can think of. Clark always looked so much slower coming through the corner and then you looked up and he'd be on pole.

What of course James had was that he could have played cricket for his county and probably England, he could have played tennis for his county and probably England, he played squash for his county. He had fantastic co-ordination. He was too big to be a runner but he was the archetypal all-round sportsman. He had timing and the other plus point – it didn't work all the time, certainly not when he went back to Harvey at Wolf – but with Harvey the first time round, Harvey had an ability to interpret James, if you know what I mean.

It's like modern [fighter] aircraft which are essentially unstable and I suspect that a really well tuned Grand Prix car, then and now, is essentially unstable because it only really performs at the sigma – final – design point. That means that it's going to perform badly unless it's driven very quickly. You can always see this. You put a less good driver in one of the cars, there was always a bigger margin. In that last part it becomes terrifically driveable.

ANN BRADSHAW

I remember all of us having dinner the night he won that race at Zandvoort, and it was great, everybody really pleased. He was in the bar, *everybody* was in the bar – none of this jumping into your hire car and rushing away immediately. Everybody was together.

ALAN JENKINS

Racing engineer

What Hesketh did was remarkable, unrepeatable – especially winning Holland – and that gave people like me the encouragement to go and have a crack with Onyx and so on. You thought it was still possible.

They were a funny mix, weren't they, the Hesketh lot? I also saw the Lord when he was a bigwig at the BRDC. Bubbles Horsley I never really knew that well. They almost over-did the *playing at it* bit. In some ways James was the most professional of them. He was a hard driver. I worked with Niki Lauda and I talked to him about James. It was something that cropped up over dinner once or twice. James always pulled Niki's leg – they were so different as personalities – but I think there was a lot of respect between them as drivers. They were great characters and if you throw the likes of Mario Andretti into that mix – well, the drivers are one-dimensional now, aren't they, in comparison?

Which brings us to Suzy Miller, the stunning blonde Hunt had been courting.

CHRIS MARSHALL

He was driving Formula 2 for me at Rouen in the early 1970s. He came down to breakfast one morning, sat at the table where my wife and I were sitting and he was looking a bit downcast. I said 'what's the matter?' He said 'I'm not sure if I've done something silly.' It turned out he'd been on the phone to her ladyship in Marbella and she'd said to him 'I've been out with so-and-so.' He said 'why? I've only been away for a few days.' She said 'he asked me out and he's really nice. And he has asked me to marry him.' James said 'well, you can't do that. I want to marry you.' So, before he knew where he was, he'd proposed, then on reflection he came down to breakfast and wasn't sure if he'd done the right thing.

ALASTAIR CALDWELL

McLaren team manager

I think the whole marriage business was Hesketh's idea anyway. James was the court jester for the Hesketh entourage and so therefore he was like a performing puppet. He had no money so he had to do something to get his drive and his something was to be the court jester for Hesketh. I believe he married Suzy because Hesketh thought it was a good idea. *Let's have a luvverly wedding, we'll all get dressed up and come to the wedding and drink champagne.* English public schoolboy marries blonde model? English public schoolboys marry blonde models all the time ...

LORD HESKETH

My idea? No, no, no-no-no. I think the truth of the matter is that James had rather changed his mind by the time he got to the church, and he wouldn't have been the first or last person to have done that and survived. He didn't survive, if you see what I mean [the marriage didn't]. He certainly said it to me on the way to the church and I said 'it's a bit late now.' It was a very big wedding. I said 'you know, everyone feels like this.' I think it's probably always easier to shift the blame onto others and I've got a broad pair of shoulders! I'm not sure that James was perfectly suited for married life really.

TAORMINA RIECK

At his engagement party to Suzy he said 'I don't know why I'm doing this.' I think he just got in too deep, frankly. It was the life he was living at the time. At the engagement party he definitely, definitely said 'I don't know why I'm doing this.' I said 'come on, be bold enough, be yourself. Just stand up and say you've made a mistake.' But I think the way things were at the time he couldn't.

J. R. RICHARDSON

We used to see each other a lot. We were mates, basically. I went to his first honeymoon, went to his first wedding! I wouldn't take it quite so far as to say the wedding was Hesketh's idea but everybody acknowledged prior to it that this was not really going to work very well. She was an absolutely sweet girl. She was very, very striking, she was very beautiful, it was the ideal couple type trip, wasn't it? But it was never going to last, really, with the life he was living. He was still up and coming, although he'd found Alexander by then. He hadn't made anything of himself but it was a wonderful time. This race team was like a party. It was terrific. They were in it for the fun and that was so evident.

Hunt and Horsley (LAT Photographic).

HUGH MACLENNAN

I did go to the Suzy wedding. It was a big, fancy affair at some church in the Brompton Road. Here I am, unknown to all these Formula 1 stars, but they were very nice and very polite. They were obviously on their best behaviour. Who am I talking about? Derek Bell, John Watson I think, Graham Hill and a few others.

Notes

1. Rentaman – a paying driver.
2. Customer cars – anyone could buy one and run it, rather than having to make a car themselves.
3. Rob Walker, paternal privateer, who ran his own team and ran Moss.
4. Barrie Gill, journalist and broadcaster, who ran a successful PR business.
5. Roger Williamson, popular Leicester driver killed in the Dutch Grand Prix at Zandvoort in 1973.

TOURIST TRAPS

A bus was parked outside Calais. If it hadn't been, a wonderfully wild chapter in James Hunt's life wouldn't have been written.

RICHARD LLOYD

My sponsor in those days was a chap called Alan Rivers – A.J. Rivers Racing, he was called – and he was a whiz kid in the property world. We're talking 30-odd years ago. He said to us one day 'come on lads, I'll borrow a car and let's go down to Monaco to have a bit of fun. We're not racing this weekend.'

So myself and one of his mates jumped into this BMW coupé, lovely summer's day in May. He was going to blast down through France and we'd have a nice weekend. Then we'd come back because we were preparing for the Tour of Britain.

This was the Avon Motor *event for saloon cars and comprised circuit races, special stages and the roads in between. It covered 1000 miles and lasted three days. Lloyd was due to driver Rivers's Chevrolet Camaro.*

We got on to the other side of the Channel, through Calais. I was sitting in the front passenger seat. It was a right-hand drive car so I was in the firing line. I remember I was reading Chapman Pincher [*Daily Express* intelligence expert]. Seat belts were really quite uncommon then and they didn't retract: you just had to grab it and get it on, and I'd managed to get it on. Alan was rattling out of Calais and I looked up, a nice, long straight road, brilliant sunshine, not a care in the world. Went back to reading Chapman Pincher and then for some reason I looked up.

What Lloyd saw was a French bus and what happened next was a not uncommon experience to British motorists of the time venturing into the embrace of French roads: a crash.

Fortunately it was a front-engined bus so all the back end was a sort of crumple zone and even more fortunately there was no-one in the back of the bus. To this day he doesn't know what happened. Anyway, I was completely winded, couldn't move. I had had the weight of the guy behind me into the back of my seat.

An ambulance came, I was the one who was incapacitated. The other two were walking wounded. We went into the hospital in Calais, the medical people checked us out and wanted to keep me. I assumed the others would stay around but not a bit of it! Alan came in, bruised and battered, and said 'right, come on Chris' – his mate. 'Richard – you all right? We're going to go on down to Monaco.' And they buggered off! There's me in a bloody hospital in Calais, which was purgatory. I couldn't move. I'd crushed two vertebrae. My girlfriend came to get me after a week and I spent another two weeks in the Royal Orthopaedic. And all this time the clock was ticking for the Tour in early July.

ROBERT FEARNALL

Journalist

I was working at *Autosport* as deputy editor. I'd known Richard Lloyd for several years and he said he was doing this Tour of Britain. A friend of his, Alan Rivers, owned the Chevrolet Camaro. They thought *if Richard is doing it would you be interested in being the co-driver?* I thought it would be a bit of fun and that's really how it started off. Richard said 'why don't we have a laugh and do this inaugural Tour of Britain?' It would be a good piece to write as well.

Then Richard was injured in a road accident going to the Monaco Grand Prix and he had damaged vertebrae. I went to see him in hospital in London and he said 'the entry's in, so why don't we get somebody else in the car?'

I can't remember whether Richard knew James well or Alan Rivers did, but they got him. I'd known James through *Autosport* days so it was no problem at all. *It'll still be a bit of a laugh and we'll carry on as is.*

James and I met only a couple of times between then and the event, then we all met up in Bath on the Thursday night for the start on Friday morning.

Hunt had driven the Camaro for the first time at Brands Hatch a couple of days before, covering only a few laps but making it go fast. Now he faced a complete array of competitors, 93 of them, from rallyman Roger Clark through to Graham Hill.

When we got off the ramp at the start we suddenly discovered that the thing had got no petrol in it so we

This chapter will be full of surprises, not least for Noel Edmonds (cartoon by Julian Kirk).

POLICE
POLICE
KIRK

had to search for the nearest petrol station. Neither James nor I had been left any money to get petrol! We thought *what the hell are we going to do when we do get to a petrol station?* We got to one and we were scrabbling around with credit cards trying to fill the blasted thing up – well, I had to do it on my credit card in the end. James wasn't going to pay for it, that was certain. I think he said '**** them, we might as well go back to the hotel.'

RICHARD LLOYD

I didn't pay James anything, I'm sure I didn't!

This Friday there was one race and three special stages before an overnight halt at Birmingham.

In the first year of the event it was very much a combination of races and a couple of hill climbs. There wasn't a great deal of competitive sections in it but there were a lot of road miles and it got a bit tedious because the Camaro wasn't the most comfortable car to drive on the road anyway.

Hunt won the race and finished the day fourth overall.

ANN BRADSHAW

I started work in the sport in late 1971 so I came across James in 1972 and he was just James, just charming. He had that ungainly walk, he showed up with his hair bedraggled, wearing tee-shirts, and that's what he was. He wasn't having any of the conformity and why should he?

I was a race organiser for the Avon and he was polite, nice, friendly because I was there to do a job. I always got on well with him and I have no negative thing I can say. He was never rude – not like Graham Hill. You had to rush round to find him to get him to sign on and things like that, but James: public school gent. I liked him. He was well educated and that shone through.

About Suzy we had no idea. James turned up in Birmingham with this beautiful blonde model on his arm. I think they'd only got a single bed in their room but he didn't seem to mind …

I was standing in reception when he walked in with her. She was absolutely beautiful, just beautiful. She looked everything that a model should look like.

BOB CONSTANDUROS

Motorsport journalist

Suzy Hunt had a sister and I shared a flat with her years and years ago. It was between Earls Court and Fulham, and the very cheapest room of the lot was really a coal hole – a basement flat under the steps. If you were very, very skint it was only £4.50 a week. I had that for a while.

I always remember seeing Suzy when he did the Tour of Britain. She was wandering round in flowing dresses and I thought *you're not going to last very long in this game, are you?* She was pretty spectacular, pretty smashing then.

The second day took them to Oulton Park.

RICHARD LLOYD

I went to one of the days on crutches, although I don't remember the famous throwing-the-gearlever-out at Oulton Park. I do know it happened! In the race there James was on his own in the car, he was leading and he started to slow. I think somebody overtook him. Then the next time round past the pits he threw something out of this bloody car at the pits. It turned out that it was the gearshift, which had broken in half. He did the rest of the race with that little stubby gearshift. He wouldn't give up, he'd bloody keep going.

After Oulton they went to Santa Pod Speedway and a 15-minute race at Silverstone.

ROBERT FEARNALL

I did some of the driving and he'd try and sleep. I got stopped once on the M6 coming out of Oulton Park for speeding. We had a bit of a laugh about that – they recognised James asleep on the back seat and there was a bit of banter. We got to Silverstone. James said 'it's a heap to drive on the road and there are so many road miles in this event. Look, Lord Hesketh's place is just down the road. Why don't I try and blow this thing up in the race, then we can all go and get pissed at Hesketh's? We can have a jolly weekend.' So I said 'well, fair enough.' He said 'you go on across to the Silverstone clubhouse and I'll see you when it's blown up.' To cut a long story short, it didn't and he won.

After the 13 laps:	
Hunt (Chevrolet Camaro)	*15m 50s*
Gordon Spice (Ford Capri)	*16m 6s*
Mike Woolley (BMW)	*16m 11s*

So then we went to Snetterton. He said 'look, we'd better take this seriously' because by the second day we were vying for the lead and all of a sudden it became a bit more of a serious proposition. Once we were in that second day and with a chance of actually winning the event, it became *let's go for it.*

It hinged on the last day and a hill climb at Dodington (a Cotswolds stately home). The stage was through a country park and James said 'right, now we're in this situation we're going to have to win this so we'll get there a bit early and I'll *run* the stage.' He'd pick me up at the other end. By then he was deadly serious. He ran through the stage taking notes of where the arrows were and all the rest of it.

We set off and on about the second corner one of the arrows warning about how tight it was had been knocked off by someone. All of a sudden we are harrying into this corner and God knows how we managed to get round it – we were all over the bleeding place – but he'd done whatever he needed to do to win the event overall and he did win it. Then we headed back to Bath and we all ended up getting exceedingly pissed in the hotel there.

I was sitting there with him for three days and he was very entertaining, told a lot of very funny stories about things that had gone on in the past. We had no back-up support or anything else. We were literally fending for ourselves as we went along. And we didn't really know what to expect.

Vintage 1973, and the Camaro at night. The first Avon Motor Tour of Britain was a combination of races and hill climbs. James felt the car was such a heap to drive on the road that the best plan was to blow it up, then he and his co-driver could go off partying for the weekend (LAT Photographic).

1, Hunt/Fearnall. 2, Spice/Stan Robinson. 3, John Handley/John Clegg (Alfa Romeo).

LORD HESKETH

I think he earned more money winning the Avon Tour of Britain in 1973 than he did driving for me for a whole season! Well, that first season – my Porsche, one of those very early RSs – lightweight – was an early payment. The Porsche disappeared. James quite liked it.

Hunt drove a Vauxhall Magnum in the 1974 Avon Tour of Britain but a piston failed. Tony Dron took part with co-driver Henry Liddon.

TONY DRON

Henry was a Monte Carlo winning co-driver. He had been very impressed by James the year before and the way he'd run the stages to see them in advance. It's perfectly within the rules but physically being able to do that was impressive and showed his commitment. He was also impressed because James saw the oil pressure dropping off at Bottom Bend, round Brands Hatch, so he had the sense to declutch through there until the pressure came back. He didn't wreck the engine and he did win the event.

In 1976, Hunt took part in the Avon Tour of Britain again. If the idea was publicity there'd be plenty of that …

ANN BRADSHAW

The first tour of Britain was a bit of fun but the event got high profile and the fun went out of it. The first one with Robert Fearnall, no hype and James went and won it. Then James was with Noel Edmonds who has always been more aware of his own image. The first time I came across him was the initial Radio 1 celebrity disc jockey race round Brands Hatch. There was DLT [Dave Lee Travis] and all the guys of those days. They were like superstars. They all came in and signed on. Noel Edmonds came in, picked up the form and *read* it. Nobody else read it. He did.

NOEL EDMONDS

TV presenter

It was an extraordinary era when you had a Formula 1 driver on his way to becoming World Champion who took part in a motor rally just before the British Grand Prix. It was fascinating. It came about because I had introduced Radio 1 to motorsport – John Webb was running Brands Hatch, Jackie Epstein running the Escort Mexicos and we used to have celebrity races. From winning a few of the celebrity races, I got an offer to go touring car racing by the wonderful Roger Willis, competitions director of Castrol. They sponsored me, I drove for Ford and Opel and it was great fun, really good. I made money at the end of the day, which was incredible. Then an opportunity came up for a Vauxhall Magnum supplied by Vauxhall – virtually a works vehicle, fairly pokey, think something off a shovel. This was at a time when Ford were very dominant so it was a marketing coup for Vauxhall. I was quite well known at the time and, although it's slightly embarrassing to say this, I was also known as a driver.

The pairing of James Hunt and myself in terms of PR appeal was seen as a bit of a dream team. I was doing the Radio 1 breakfast show, which was getting 14 to 15 million listeners – we are talking pre commercial radio – and I remember on the Friday morning before the rally started I did my show from the Birmingham Post House. Then we got in this car and off we went. I was navigating and James did all the driving. The Tour of Britain was a mixture of circuits – where the nominated driver drove alone in a race – and rally stages where you had a navigator, and so it was my job to make sure the car was ready for the actual races and to get James in the right place at the right time, which was not easy.

I'd met him at a few things but I didn't know him, so the image came way ahead of the man. I remember him being extraordinarily rude to my wife. My wife Gill was a very, very important part of our support team. Gill used to come to all my motor races and she really loved motor racing. Of course she thought James Hunt was wonderful but he was a sexist bastard and he just didn't take on board that she was important to me and important to what we were doing.

However, that said, I found him in all of the promotional work we did building up to it – the PR and the photographs – really patient, *really* patient, really co-operative. I've read quite a bit about James and I can

The ride to the limit and beyond, with Noel Edmonds in the 1976 Tour of Britain (LAT Photographic).

247m
RADIO 1
VAUXHALL
WXE 935M

TEXACO
KANGOL
WXE 935M

WXE 935M

understand why some people come to negative conclusions, but my whole feeling towards him was one of great positivity and respect for what he was doing. He was his own man.

The fact that he was so professional and yet rude to my wife does fit together because, in my experience, he only did what James wanted to do, so he was actually very interested in radio. He got a buzz about coming to Broadcasting House and doing the photos, and he hung around the studios and was generally interested.

I don't say I was in awe of him, because for me he can't hold a candle to my real heroes such as Clark and Jackie Stewart and Graham Hill, the last two of whom I met. James was a very different sort of hero racing driver but he did love to turn up in appalling clothes at formal occasions. There was that side to him and therefore I wasn't surprised – and Gill wasn't particularly upset – that he just seemed to delight in dismissing her involvement and her presence.

That said, this was an extraordinary event we took part in and of course we didn't stay in it for very long!

The bit on the road where the police were involved was actually worse than it was reported. We were chased by the police and I remember us driving down public roads at in excess of 120, 130 miles an hour and I was so cripplingly ashamed of what was happening that I tried to have my arm out of the car covering my name – because all the people we were cutting up, no, I mean scything – there were people ending up on pavements and all sorts of thing – the only name they would have seen was mine, painted on the side of the car.

I can remember at one point in Lincolnshire, we were piling down this long straight road. I was trying to reach for my crash helmet, which was on the rack at the back of this thing, because I thought *we are going to die – something terrible is going to happen.* If only to hide my embarrassment I was going to put it on.

The whole thing was quite phenomenal.

He didn't actually drive very well, it has to be said. Now that's pretty grand coming from me, isn't it? It's the transition from tarmac to rally stage. Very few have done it: very, very few. People talk about Jim Clark as one of the few who did both. Even Martin Brundle has failed to make a mark in rallies. James was not good at driving on the loose stuff. The tree we hit you would have missed and I would have missed. We'd have hit one of the other trees because we were in a bloody forest. When we went into this tree, it was a phenomenal experience – he hit it absolutely square on.

The stage we were on was an old ammunition dump in a forest in Norfolk, and they were old tarmac roads from the Second World War. But the Ordnance Survey map of it was totally accurate, and although we weren't meant to be having notes and things at this particular time, one of the other navigators said to me 'trust the OS map, it's right' and I had spoken to one or two people from the Forestry Commission before we started about the stage – I talked it through with them – and they said 'that is accurate'. So I said to James 'look, I'll call the corners and trust me, I believe it's right.' Now there were arrows and things. We piled off into this forest and I know I got it right. We came down this straight bit and I said '90 right'. He was on the brakes and we just went straight into this bloody big tree. We hit it so hard and so square that if we'd had a rear seat passenger he could have changed the gears for us. The engine came into the cockpit – a phenomenal thud and we were out of the rally.

I think he was really embarrassed. The stories all went that he stormed off, and this, that and the other, but I think he was just acutely embarrassed. Now, in his defence, I think his mind was on the World Championship and the forthcoming British Grand Prix. And I don't think he was having fun. It wasn't James's sort of fun to try and drive a Vauxhall through a forest. I was heartbroken because I wanted to promote the whole Radio 1 thing and I wanted to get to the end, but underneath I think he was quite pleased it happened.

Because what seems to emerge is that people of that calibre want to control the vehicle at all times and of course good rally drivers arrive at the corner, have the accident first and then drive round the corner. That is alien, I think, to really good circuit drivers.

RICHARD LLOYD

The rider to all this, just to complete the circle, is that dear old Alan and I are still good friends. It was he who rang up – we were discussing things about six months ago [2005] – and he said 'I know what would be fun. Why

A life in headlines, Avon Tour of Britain 1973 – that's Autosport Deputy Editor Robert Fearnall beside Hunt and (below) Hunt with Noel Edmonds in 1976 (Autosport).

don't we get the Camaro back and do some races?' I said 'we can do one better than that. I can't find the car but there's a friend of mine who's starting an event called Tour Britannia, which is based loosely on the Tour of Britain.' So Alan said 'right, that's it, we're going to find a car and we're going to re-create it in the exact colours and do it again.' And that's what we are doing in September this year. So that'll be a little memory of James Hunt.

There's a footnote, too, about Hunt's approach – sometimes, anyway – to driving on the roads.

SARAH LOMAX

Second wife

We were going to a pro-am at Gleneagles, don't ask me what year, in the old brown 6.9 Merc. It didn't always go but it went that night, went like a rocket. We left at about 11 o'clock at night from Wimbledon and near the Scottish borders there was a police car, a Panda car, behind us. So he thought *no, I'm not going to stop for that one* and he put his foot down. It was a bit hairy. We got well in front and he pulled off onto a track. We hid behind bushes and watched the Panda go by. You could almost feel the Panda's driver saying *where's he going, where's he going, where's he gone?* We then came out and James really put his foot down, overtook the Panda. James said he knew it was the changeover at the border and the Panda car couldn't follow. *It will take him a little while to phone through and get another guy on the other side to pick us up.* Well, we were gone – and in thick fog.

They were chasing us and we were doing 120 miles an hour in this fog, three o'clock in the morning. He said 'the best place for you is down there on the floor – lie down, think of England and don't forget I'm the highest paid chauffeur in the world.' We got away. His concentration! I'll never forget seeing the veins and the muscles on his forearms. I felt actually OK. He said 'don't look at the needle.' Afterwards I was fine but Oscar [the dog] was ill for days ...

Although not well-suited to the narrow stage, James Hunt's Camaro established an excellent time at Knebworth only 3 s slower than fastest

TOUR OF BRITAIN

James Hunt in Camaro takes hard-fought win

By JOHN DAVENPORT and ROBERT FEARNALL
Pictures by COLIN TAYLOR PRODUCTIONS

That man Hunt again

By all accounts, Naughty Boy of the Tour award on the Texaco Tour of Britain would surely go to Texaco driver James Hunt. Rumours of dices with Lord Hesketh's Rolls Royce, putting people off the road, giving V signs to drivers waving at the 247 Radio One Magnum, excessive road speed, arguments with co-driver Noel Edmonds, evading the police. . . . all these were rumours circulating the Great Barr Post House, quite apart from the fact that he might have been booked for three different road infringments, including dangerous driving.

However, the more official story goes along these lines. Firstly, before the event started, Hunt was required to run on Goodyear tyres which he found to be insufficient for the job, and was later to annoy him. Then on the way to Silverstone, he had an altercation with a Rolls which had been tailgating the Magnum, and later, a co-driver's mistake caused him to turn in front of another motorist which upset the man, and he later phoned the Tour organizers to complain.

After Hunt's "off" in Norfolk, he was reportedly upset with the performance of the car and wished to retire, but Edmonds considered they had a duty to his listeners and urged Hunt to continue. DTV repaired the Magnum, but they were well behind time. The road section from Norfolk to Lincolnshire was tight and crowded anyway so that to travel at illegal speeds was probably the only way to stay in the event without going over time allowed.

Police activity in Lincolnshire was considerable and Hunt was reportedly picked up for speeding. He arrived at the Cadwell control just within time with a police car on his tail, but Jim McRae moved his SMT Magnum out of line for the control and blocked the police car, so they were unable to catch Hunt. They waited for him to reappear but the exit was at a different place to the entrance and ultimately they caught up with the Magnum at the end of the next stage, Ludford. As spectators were crowding around the car asking for autographs, the police took Hunt a few miles down the road where they interviewed him for around 17 minutes about the speeding offence and the lack of lights caused by the accident. When Edmonds joined up with Hunt, DTV set to repair the lights, but by this stage, it was going to mean another rapid run to the next special stage, and Hunt was unwilling to be put in the same position again, so they retired there and then.

Silly. James Hunt, egged on by Noel Edmonds(l), has yet another moment in front of the public eye on last weekend's Texaco Tour of Britain.

Marlboro
Marlboro
TEXACO

RAT CATCHER

He'd driven in 36 Grands Prix, all for Hesketh. He'd been on the front row a couple of times, won Zandvoort and scored, in context, an impressive 62 points. Then, approaching 1976, something completely unexpected happened and it literally opened up the world.

This chapter is not a series of race reports covering that season but, rather, people's strong memories of it. There were various bans, protests and appeals along the way which often rendered championship positions provisional – and a nightmare to grasp. I have simplified it by giving points as they became after all the protesting, and only for Hunt, driving a McLaren, and the man he ultimately defeated, Niki Lauda (Ferrari), known affectionately as The Rat.

TEDDY MAYER

McLaren team boss

We got James at the very last minute because we'd been hoping to do a deal with Emerson, or renew our deal with Emerson, and he decided finally to set up his own team. So James was very much, to be honest, what was available at the time. We were both pleasantly surprised when he put the car on pole in Brazil. Up to that moment I don't think he did know how good he was.[1] Hesketh was an interesting sort of phenomena because some days they were very quick and some days they were very slow. We looked on it more as a science.

James was a very complex guy as well as a talented driver. He came from a different sort of family background from a normal race driver and, having been through the Hesketh situation, he had some pre-conceived ideas of which we eventually disabused him. He thought that – it's very difficult to say, but he thought racing was a sport and not a business, which it had been with Hesketh. Well, I assume so, anyway. Whereas driving for McLaren and Marlboro we had maybe a different outlook on it and on life. We were in the business of winning races and championships – but I got the impression that when Hesketh and James won in Holland that was a kind of peak. They were not in the business of taking on Ferrari for the World Championship.

We'd had very professional drivers and I think at first James was not a very professional driver but over the course of the year he came to understand that we had to perform day in and day out and he changed quite a lot, actually, in terms of his approach to it.

The McLaren nucleus. Hunt with team manager Alastair Caldwell (left) and team boss Teddy Mayer (LAT Photographic).

BRIAN HENTON

Make no mistake, it looked like the Hesketh team were all playboys but with Postlethwaite they were a very talented little bunch. I am sure the Hesketh period gave James a licence to become even more eccentric. What he'd done, he'd actually created his own image and it quite suited Marlboro at that time for them to have the unorthodox playboy in the team.

And he was just like that.

J. R. RICHARDSON

They called me The Kid because I used to wear cowboy boots and a funny hat. If you were around James, nobody noticed! It was funny. You know The Weiner [Mayer's nickname]? I met him in a hotel in Surrey I suppose six, seven, eight years ago – a chance meeting – and we had a chat. He said 'I spent a long time trying to figure out whether your group and your presence helped James drive better or actually hindered him. I came to the conclusion that it helped his performance because it gave him some sort of stability, some sort of context.' I was pleased to hear that. We hung around because we were interested in a friend's progress within his chosen field, where he was doing well. We never exploited it or anything like that. We showed up and we were in the way. We used to sit around the Marlboro hospitality bit. We weren't really welcome because we didn't have a part to play although I ran the hospitality once at Jarama.

Despite their intense battle on the track, Niki Lauda was Hunt's friend as well as rival and made the 1976 season immortal (LAT Photographic).

That's as close as I got! But we felt like outsiders who were eventually welcome. Hogan was pretty good like that. There were, I suppose, three or four of us.

ALASTAIR CALDWELL

McLaren team manager

James was forced on us, there was no option. He rang us up and said *I think I'm your Grand Prix driver* and we said *yeah, we guess you're right.* Mrs. Hesketh got peed off with her boy spending all the money and closed the race team down. We lost Fittipaldi because he went off and created his own race team, which [sponsor] Philip Morris hadn't allowed for. They thought they had him by the balls in negotiations because he had nowhere else to go – but he did, so suddenly we had no racing driver and James had no seat. So we were thrust upon each other and history will tell you: pole for his first race. We went to Brazil with no testing at all – well, we went to Silverstone in the snow and the rain and checked out that he could reach

the pedals and so on. We'd had to modify the car because he had long legs and a short arse – the Hunchback of Colnbrook, as he was known. He was a very odd-shaped fellow: real short body and long legs. But he was quick, and he was funny; and being quick and funny was quite useful.

Hunt, partnered by Jochen Mass, faced Niki Lauda and Clay Regazzoni in the Ferraris, Jody Scheckter and Patrick Depailler in the Tyrrells, Mario Andretti and Ronnie Peterson in the Lotuses.

Brazil, 25 January: Hunt pole, podium Lauda, Depailler, Tom Pryce (Shadow) – Hunt accident. Lauda 9, Hunt 0.

I wasn't interested in journalists – in fact I was anti journalists in general. Mostly they were idiots and ignorant of their subject, so they always irritated me. I shouldn't have allowed that, I should have just talked to them because that was one of McLaren's failings in those days. We didn't have a PR man, we didn't make Press Releases, we didn't talk to journalists. We had a very limited number of people and we went motor racing – which was the least of the things you need. The one thing you don't need is results. What you need is bullshit and we were just low on bullshit – but good on results. It's just a fact. You can go for years and years with no results as long as you have good bullshit. People aren't interested in results, only bullshit. The ideal combination is both.

They were about to get both. South Africa, 6 March: Hunt pole, podium Lauda, Hunt, Mass. Lauda 18, Hunt 6.

One thing about James, he was never boring. He was always interesting to have around, and he was a very quick racing driver, which is what teams like. There's no doubt he was quick. He might not have been the world's best racing driver – because he wasn't the complete animal, he wasn't your Prost or your Lauda or your Schumacher or your Piquet because he wasn't hard-working enough to do all the rest of the stuff. But he was very quick. So he was a good qualifier and a good racer, he just wasn't a good tester and he wasn't a good PR man. Well, he was a bit, in that the sponsors loved him because he was controversial – the tee-shirts, jeans, bare feet, all

Hunt's team-mates: Jochen Mass ... and Patrick Tambay (LAT Photographic).

that. They all liked a bit of drama in their lives.

That was helped by the fact that his missus ran off with [actor] Richard Burton, and that contributed to his fame. James's publicity overhang I never found a problem. If journalists wanted to get in a fever over his missus running off, that was never really a problem. They were a bit of a problem, however, when they rang you up at three o'clock in the morning and ambushed you. God, they were hard. I always feel sympathy for people who get involved.

The drivers' briefing in South Africa, stormy second Grand Prix of the 1976 season: Andretti, Mass and Hunt share a joke in the second row. Note Ken Tyrrell and Bernie Ecclestone, directly behind Andretti, and Max Mosley standing behind Mass, enjoying the joke too (LAT Photographic).

When they want to harass you they are just magnificent at it. They are champions at asking the question that has no answer. You can't say no comment, you can't say yes and you can't say no. James had it all his life. He coped quite well with it and enjoyed it, in fact. I don't remember James moaning too much about Press attention.

He'd had this with Hesketh, hadn't he? So he was used to it before he came to us. Nobody said *Jesus Christ, the Press is hounding us this week.*

South Africa was when Suzy first went off with Burton so we actually had to hide him. We got a South African tennis player who took James off to his house and hid him there – took him away in a small car at the end of the day. We were staying at a local hotel – the Sleepy Hollow, a very nice little hotel we went to by mistake

Why today's big reconciliation between James and Suzy Hunt has gone for a Burton . . .

PLANS for a reconciliation between James Hunt and his model wife Suzy in London this week have been cancelled and divorce talk, which I revealed two weeks ago, is now going ahead.

Suzy, 27, is remaining with Richard Burton while James, who failed by 1.3 seconds to win the South African Grand Prix at the weekend, is flying to London to stay with his former patron, Lord Hesketh.

'She is not returning to London to meet her husband,' Brook Williams, executive aide to Burton, tells me. 'There are no plans for her to leave—it is her first visit to New York and she is finding it very exciting.'

The Hunts parted a month ago after arranging to meet again today. But in

Staying: Suzy

Hunt hits front at 120 mph

JOHANNESBURG Thursday

BRITAIN'S James Hunt proved to himself and the rest of the Formula One motor-racing fraternity that he really is capable of becoming the world's top driver.

In one of the most sensational practice sessions in recent Grand Prix racing, 28-year-old Hunt played a cat and mouse game with World Champion Niki Lauda and emerged with the major prize—pole position on the grid for Saturday's South African G.P. at the Kyalami track.

Hunt has been hounded by the South African Press over his wife Susy's personal life. But, with just an hour left of official practice, he told me: "I would really like to give them something else to write about this afternoon."

He was as good as his word.

Weekend Argus

IT'S LAUDA ALL THE WAY AT KYALAMI

From Keith Macfarlane

KYALAMI. — Niki Lauda, the 27-year-old world champion won the South African Grand Prix for Ferrari today at an average speed of 187.73 km/h from James Hunt (McLaren), Jochen Mass (McLaren) and Jody Scheckter (Tyrrell).

A life in headlines. By South Africa, Hunt's marriage was over and Suzy had gone off with Richard Burton. Lauda won the Grand Prix from Hunt by 1.3 seconds … Now Hunt's marriage was food for the gossip columnists such as (left) Nigel Dempster in the Daily Mail.

once and never left! It's right out by the racetrack. And nobody knew we were there: we were anti publicity, we were anti journalists – which was just so stupid, because that's where the money is.

I just knew that suddenly we had huge media interest. We had the *Sydney Morning Herald* on the expletive telephone, and the *Punjabi Times*, we had every daily newspaper in the world – Mexico, even! – all trying to interview us and talk to James. They were being flown in by the planeload. So James went off with this tennis player, very nice house, and played tennis. Then when he turned up at the track we could muscle them out of the pit road and keep him more or less isolated and then he'd go off again. But he loved every minute of it.

CHRIS MARSHALL

Suzy said she thoroughly enjoyed going racing because James always won, which was true, but right from the word go the marriage wasn't perfect and after a while he said to her 'look, you need to be kept in the manner to which you have become accustomed and the best thing is for you to find somebody who can do that.' So he paid to pack her off to St. Moritz with a friend and she saw Richard Burton in the ski queue and accidentally collided with him. He picked her up and took one look at her, took her into the 'egg' going up the mountain and by the time they got to the top they were off and running. James was actually delighted. It worked out brilliantly. James, of course, was *désolé* in public and everybody was on his side but in fact he was rubbing his hands together because it didn't cost him anything. What a fairytale story! He wasn't upset about her going off with Burton.

All of which leads to a funny episode years later when his second marriage was ending …

SARAH LOMAX

James said 'go to Verbiers, I'll pay and if you do as well as Suzy we'll be all right!' He really did say that. Hilarious. That was so *him* and he didn't mean it in a nasty way. That was his humour and totally genuine and there was no reason not to find it terribly amusing. I came back. He said 'how did you get on?' I said 'I didn't do very well, I found a rather sad penniless Italian count.' He said 'well, you'd better come in!'

Anyway, back to 1976 …

USA West, 28 March. Pole Regazzoni, podium Regazzoni, Lauda, Depailler – Hunt accident. Lauda 24, Hunt 6.

Spain, 2 May, Jarama. Pole Hunt, podium Hunt, Lauda, Gunnar Nilsson (Lotus). After the race, Hunt was disqualified – the car fractionally too wide – and McLaren appealed. Eventually Hunt was reinstated. Lauda 30, Hunt 15.

JOCHEN MASS

Driver

Dear old James. Already in 1976 he was a rebel without a cause. He wore tennis shoes with the Tuxedo top and made himself unpopular at times. I knew him from Formula 3 days so we actually had quite a few little adventures in London together. I'm not talking about racing, I'm talking about privately … about London nights. That's where we got to know each other reasonably well. And you had to go and see the doctor …!

There was a girl called Mercedes and she worked for Spanish television. She said 'can I do an interview?' He said 'not a problem' and they stood him beside the camera. And as she was asking him a question he asked her 'do you ****?' She said 'thank you James' and walked off. Sometimes he just went over the edge with statements and things like that. He was an eccentric. I think he tried to live up to this sort of pop star idol in England, which they made of him.

Maybe he never realised this was pretty phoney, but later in life he came round and was a lot more normal. I mean, he was still wild because he never shook it off completely. On the other hand, had he not died in this unfortunate way he would have become a pretty solid human being. I met Rod Stewart and Mick Jagger and a lot of footballers, Malcolm Macdonald and some of the other guys and I could see where it came from. You have a lot of footballers who go wrong because they can't take the pressure, but James was good with that. He could live up to that. He just searched for something within himself, he was constantly running after something. I don't know whether he knew what it was. He was a fair team-mate, he was favoured certainly by McLaren in the English style.

JOHN BLUNSDEN

Correspondent, The Times

He was a very intelligent bloke. This is one of the mysteries: why an intelligent bloke would abuse himself to the extent that he did. There's no doubt about it, he got in with the wrong set. There were a lot of them around at that time, who were prepared to play harder than was wise. If he hadn't been such a fit and athletic bloke initially then frankly I don't think he would have made the grade in motor racing. He obviously had very good reactions, his sense of co-ordination was good, despite the drugs, but notwithstanding that, as we all know, he perhaps had some difficulty in knowing where the limit was because he had quite a few fairly spectacular shunts on his way up. Hunt the Shunt exactly. To that extent his judgement was not perhaps 100% – probably 99% – but fundamentally he was a brave bloke and he drove hard.

I think the eye-opener to me was that Spanish Grand Prix where the Spaniards had cocked things up yet again. There was usually some sort of cock-up in the Spanish Grand Prix. This time it was the fact that they didn't have the medical helicopter and Bernie & Co. rightly said *there's no way we are going to start without it.* This was practice, not the race. So we were all there twiddling our thumbs for an hour while the Spaniards started to build a helicopter, I suppose!

I was just walking up and down the pit road, I landed in his pit and we started chatting. It wasn't about motor racing, it was about things in general. I knew that he had a place over in Spain and I think I probably opened the conversation by saying 'you can always get on your bike and cycle home.' I said 'what's it like over here?' and he said 'well, it's great.' He'd opened up this bar and he'd got his own pad and he was talking property terms. He said 'wise people really should be investing their money not in expensive toys but in important things like property.' He was even considering a farm at that stage. I don't know whether he had a particularly strong interest in farming or whether he thought it was a good investment.

It was very much Hunt the businessman and Hunt looking at the wider world beyond Grand Prix. I thought that was quite refreshing, because even then there weren't too many people who could see beyond the rear wing and the nosecone, could see there was a big life out there. I certainly felt that his head was well and truly screwed on properly – bearing in mind he hadn't won the World Championship. At that stage he'd done nothing much that year and nobody knew he was going to win it. He wasn't a championship contender, really.

It was nice to be able to talk about other things and to get genuine, considered opinion from a driver. We must have been chatting for over an hour. I would say he was very perceptive and I sense that when he jumped into McLaren – after Fittipaldi left unexpectedly – they had the right sort of business-like attitude to everything. They could never have been accused of wasting money or encouraging their drivers to waste any money! I wouldn't be surprised if they didn't point him in the right direction. They were in the business of winning championships and he'd taken that on board. From being the clown in the Hesketh regime he had allowed himself to be changed, if you like. Perhaps more of the genuine Hunt came out.

Belgium, 16 May. Pole Lauda, podium Lauda, Regazzoni, Jacques Laffite (Ligier) – Hunt transmission failure. Lauda 39, Hunt 15.

Monaco, 30 May. Pole Lauda, podium Lauda, Scheckter, Depailler – Hunt engine failure. Lauda 48, Hunt 15.

Sweden, 13 June. Pole Scheckter, podium Scheckter, Depailler, Lauda – Hunt fifth. Lauda 52, Hunt 17.

France, 4 July. Pole Hunt, podium Hunt, Depailler, John Watson (Penske). Lauda 52, Hunt 26.

Britain, 18 July. Pole Lauda, podium Lauda, Scheckter, Watson. A crash halted the race and Hunt, his McLaren damaged, limped back to the pits using the lane from the back of the track – so he didn't complete a lap. While officials debated whether he should be excluded from the re-start the crowd boiled. He did take the re-start but was subsequently disqualified. Lauda 61, Hunt 26.

BRIAN JONES

Brands Hatch commentator

My first Grand Prix commentary was in 1976 when, somewhat inadvertently, we nearly caused a riot. I was up in the box in Westfield [a bend out in the country] and I had alongside me Keith Douglas, there as an RAC steward, who'd also been a commentator for years. Because it was my first Grand Prix it was quite special to me and I wanted to call every driver through as they went round on the opening lap – as a matter of pride. This I was determined to do and I was vaguely aware of Anthony Marsh [the main commentator] booming in the background 'and the race has been stopped'. I was saying 'now here's Depailler' and whoever else it was – I called them through anyway.

Hunt, half naked but wholly unaffected by being reduced to pedal power (Peter Brooker/Rex Features).

The mood at the 1976 British Grand Prix, when 77,000 spectators booed and cheered and raged as the fortunes of their local hero kept changing (LAT Photographic).

The whole thing was stopped and James, of course, made the cardinal error of going through the hairpin, down through Graham Hill bend and, using local knowledge, nipped in through the back door, that little lane up to the paddock. That was what cost him the race, although of course we didn't know at the time. Keith was sitting alongside me and he had a copy of the yellow book[2] and so, while Anthony was trying to play everything down, we wound everything up – because, like the rest of the crowd, we wanted Hunt to be able to start again. Anthony was saying 'well, I don't think we should speculate any more' and we were saying 'well, there's every good reason why James Hunt should be allowed to start again.' We had no idea about the response of the crowd over on the club circuit side but in the end the message began to filter through.

I do remember I took my kids to that Grand Prix and we must have known something because we took a bottle of champagne and some glasses. When the race was over and James *had* won – as far as we were concerned – we stood at the edge of the track, and there wasn't another soul in sight. In those days the drivers on the podium used to come round [on the back of a truck] doing a lap of honour and we toasted him in champagne as he went by. He acknowledged us – of course he did! He'd have had a glass himself if the driver had stopped, you can be sure of that!

JOHN WEBB

Owner, Brands Hatch

There was indeed nearly a riot. In fact Angela, who'd just been made a director by then, recalls that we were approached by the police who said 'you are about to have a riot on your hands.' That was really because the late Anthony Marsh didn't give the crowd the right sort of information. He got them in a rebellious state [*but see Brian Jones, above!*] and the police were quite anxious at that time. We couldn't do anything about it. We were the circuit owners but the meeting was being run by the RAC. I don't think we regarded it as terribly serious because British crowds at motor race meetings don't get out of control. It was purely the James Hunt factor. If it had been any two other drivers nobody would have bothered too much.

Incidentally, the whole race meeting had to be run on a generator because one of the visiting helicopters flew into power cables – so if we hadn't had a big stand-by generator for the first time the whole incident wouldn't have happened because there wouldn't have been a race.

Germany, 1 August. Pole, Hunt, podium Hunt, Scheckter, Mass. Lauda crashed and almost burnt to death but by superhuman willpower returned at the Italian Grand Prix. Lauda 61, Hunt 35.

SIMON TAYLOR

When James moved to McLaren I was doing BBC radio single-handed in those days and it involved my going to races, doing the commentary and then the interviews afterwards. He was difficult, because once he got to McLaren he'd become extremely serious about his racing. He wanted to win the World Championship and during the years at McLaren one saw less of his well-known public school image. There was some of that but basically, while he was still struggling with the McLaren when he first went there, he was very, very serious about it. He wore his curious clothes – tee-shirts and bare feet – but he *was* very serious.

When things were going well one could go and sit at the McLaren motorhome and have a very intelligent and in-depth conversation about how the car was behaving. He was unusual in that he didn't just get in the car and drive it, he particularly thought about other drivers and their strengths and weaknesses. He attacked it in a very intellectual way, and it was rare then. Now you have other people to do it for you.

Then it was new, and the reason why James and Niki became complete friends – and they really were very, very good mates – was because James and Niki saw in each other the same level of intelligence, which was considerably higher than the average intelligence of most of the other drivers. You'd have somebody like Ronnie who just drove brilliantly because he didn't know how to do anything else but you couldn't ask him to come and analyse what was going on.

Although they were always driving for different teams, and for a long time actually were rivals for the championship, they maintained this good humoured, friendly respect for each other. They used to go and have dinner together at Grands Prix. It would be like Kimi

The extraordinary home race, which Hunt won and lost (LAT Photographic).

So who needs rules?

MERVYN EDGECOMBE ON THE GRAND PRIX WORLD

Hunt stays away from star-makers

'If I didn't get away from it all I'd just crack up'

Daily Mail

An amazing Grand Prix win for Britain after race team repair crashed car

JAMES HUNT SUPER STAR

A life in headlines – the row over Hunt's victory at Brands Hatch was hot news not just in Autosport or on the sports features but as front page lead in the Fleet Street dailies.

Räikkönen having dinner with Fernando Alonso and enjoying it and talking about art or music or girls or whatever. You couldn't imagine this happening now, never mind it being natural.

That was what James was like when things were going well. He was much more tweaked up than people realised. When things were going badly you got behind the laid back, devil-may-care, dashing sort of image which implied – to people who didn't know him very well – that he was like an old fashioned RAF spitfire pilot. You saw, in fact, how very, very serious about it he really was when things had gone badly.

I had an agreement that I'd go and see him 20 minutes after the race. They didn't have Press Conferences then, you've got to remember. I had to get to James and do a minute and a half about his race with him. He was the big British hero. It was partly because of James that I persuaded the BBC radio that they ought to start taking motorsport seriously. If he'd had a bad race I'd go up and talk to him and he'd be monosyllabic or tell me to *eff off*. He'd be so upset about how things had gone – so he was far more emotionally involved than you might have thought.

Austria, 15 August. Pole, Hunt, podium Watson, Laffite, Nilsson – Hunt fourth. Lauda 61, Hunt 38.

Holland, 29 August. Pole, Peterson, podium, Hunt, Regazzoni, Andretti. Lauda 61, Hunt 47.

JOHN WATSON

My view of James Hunt as a fellow driver? He was naturally very fast and he was obviously an intelligent man. He was a tough racer. I had archetypal races with James in 1976 and 1977. At Zandvoort in '77 I had a car which was quicker over a whole lap but he had a car which was fractionally quicker down the straight because we were running different levels of downforce. He successfully defended his position, which he did with a fair degree of firmness. It was a classic duel of two Brits in Formula 1.

[In *Grand Prix!*[5] Mike Lang writes: '... on lap 27 the two cars went into Tarzan side by side. There they stayed all the way around the hairpin but by sitting it out on the racing line Hunt staved off the challenge while Watson, after putting his near-side wheels over the outside kerbing and briefly into the sand, fell in behind once more. But this proved to be just the beginning of one of the finest duels seen for a long time as during the next half hour Watson made repeated attempts, both at the hairpin and elsewhere, to force his way into the lead.']

Italy, 12 September. Pole, Laffite, podium, Peterson, Regazzoni, Laffite – Lauda fourth, Hunt did not finish. Lauda 64, Hunt 47.

Canada, 3 October. Pole, Hunt, podium, Hunt, Depailler, Andretti – Lauda eighth. Lauda 64, Hunt 56.

TEDDY MAYER

I remember when we were practising for the Canadian Grand Prix at Mosport and Tyler Alexander[4] was running our Indy team at the time. He came up and watched James driving in practice and he said he looks quicker than anybody else – and I think James was quick but he also knew it was very dangerous.

How, running a team, do you go about that? We kind of left him to himself, and I think that was what he wanted. He wanted to be left alone to deal with it, which he did very well most times. If he hadn't sorted it out by himself, I can't think what we could have done to help him. He was very much his own man and you certainly couldn't dissuade him from believing it was dangerous. On the other hand, I don't think you could just tell him not to drive, either. It was always his decision.

Unhappy Monza, for many reasons (LAT Photographic).

A DOG'S LIFE

JOHN WATSON

The side of James I focus on was when he became a father, but also with Oscar the Alsatian. In my perception of James he had, basically, two sides. There was a very loving, caring man and I first saw it in the manner in which he and his beloved Oscar related. It was one man and his dog.

Very often people are better able to express their emotions through inanimate objects, or something like a dog, than in a normal one-on-one human relationship. I understand that very well. A dog is dependent – and a cat is independent. I'm not a cat lover, I'm a dog lover. James had a relationship with Oscar that a human being might not give you. I'd seen other sides of James but I noticed this side when he was with Oscar.

Also when James was living down in Spain – life down there on your own, in spite of having girlfriends trolling up and down, wasn't a barrel of laughs in reality. At Marbella he must have had people hanging on to him because he was James Hunt. Sunshine is wonderful but, if you have no particular purpose sitting in it, it can be pretty damn awful.

ALAN JENKINS

We got talking about dogs one day. We had a German Shepherd which wasn't quite as big as his and we also had a Jack Russell. And our Jack Russell ended up co-habiting with his – ours male, his female – and we ended up socialising, well, in a bizarre set of meetings on hard shoulders of motorways exchanging dogs. I went to his house a few times towards the end of his life.

We got to the point where he'd say 'I'm going to drive to this race, why don't you come?' He'd load up a carrier bag full of tape cassettes and instead of flying I sat alongside him and listen to obscure tapes of the musical influences he was keen on at the time.

JO JENKINS

Wife of Alan

I think the year was 1985. We'd got to know James in the McLaren days but Alan had left to go to [American team] Penske. There was very much a 'family' atmosphere then

Hunt had a very loving, caring side, which some insiders first saw in the way in which he and his beloved Oscar related (LAT Photographic).

which the sponsors, Philip Morris, helped to cultivate at McLaren. In the motorhome hospitality area at the end of a long day people would chat and have the opportunity to get to know each other. This resulted in a feeling of being part of a strong team.

James and Sarah had a very small Jack Russell terrier bitch called Muffi. They decided that she should have some puppies. James knew that we had a Jack Russell and a German Shepherd, as had he. Our 'JR' was called Gus, he was a proven dad and had the most fantastic temperament. So Gus was chosen to do the deed.

Like many small bitches, Muffi proved to be difficult to breed from so, to help things along, it was decided that Gus should go and stay at James's house in Wimbledon. This would mean that when/if Muffi was in the mood Gus would be on hand. His visit started *really* well because when he had been in James's sitting room five minutes maximum he peed on the leg of the TV!

Fortunately both James and Sarah were animal lovers with a great sense of humour and all was forgiven. Muffi had a 'headache' throughout the duration of the stay and nothing was achieved. However Gus proved very useful at exercising James's show budgerigars. These were kept in a very large aviary and Gus would trot quietly from one end of the aviary to the other, watching them as they flew from left to right. This was evidently useful, as otherwise the birds got too big and fat.

About a month later I was returning to our home in the New Forest having dropped Alan at Heathrow. When he was with Penske Racing he was commuting to the States and I would take him to the airport and collect him from it – this helped him to be marginally less exhausted! At the time I was driving a Mercedes 'G' Wagon. There were very few on the road in the UK so I had got used to it causing a fair bit of interest.

On this particular trip I was not hanging about driving along the M3 extension when I was aware of a male in a smart saloon car dodging backwards and forwards behind me. Like any lone woman driver, I ignored him.

I then got the flashing headlights – I ignored it.

I then got the overtaking and suddenly slowing down routine – I ignored it.

I then got the pulling level and hovering level with me routine – I ignored it.

I was not going to make eye contact, but then I thought 'sod it, let's see if this jerk can lip read!' As I turned to my right I had a shock: there was the laughing face of James Hunt ...

He waved at me to pull over, which I duly did. He jumped out and we caused quite a few drivers to rub their eyes in disbelief – there was the ex Formula 1 World Champion and well-known TV commentator standing at the side of the road chatting to petite blonde! Muffi had come into season that morning and James had tried phoning our house but got no reply so he figured that by the time he had driven down to our house I would be back and he could collect Gus. Fortunately Gus was with me so we exchanged him and off he whizzed with James.

Sadly nothing came of this doggy liaison, but it left us with yet another great memory of a lovely man.

ALAN JENKINS

James always had this old style Merc, one with a huge engine. The transfer of dogs took place on the hard shoulder of the M3. You could *not* imagine things like that happening with anybody else.

USA, 10 October. Pole, Hunt, podium, Hunt, Scheckter, Lauda. Lauda 68, Hunt 65 – and only Mount Fuji, Japan remaining.

ALASTAIR CALDWELL

I took the team to Japan testing, against Teddy's express orders.

On the Sunday night after the US Grand Prix I organised a truck to come from New York to pick the car up on Monday morning, because the only freighter that could take the car to Japan went on Monday night. When I helped Teddy down to the helicopter he said to me 'I know that in the back of your mind you've got this idea of taking a car to Japan and I don't want that done.' I said 'yeah, yeah, right.' I already had the truck on the way.

I sent the car to Japan.

James flew out with me. We went down to New York, caught a plane together with two mechanics and went to Japan. So I fooled Ferrari and got the car there. We spent a week trying to get the car through customs, which was a big effort. We tried to test the Saturday before the Grand Prix, which in those days was the rule. You had to test one week before. Unfortunately the car broke down after a few laps but it was still a fantastic deal for James because James was totally orientated to Japan by the time the race started. He'd seen the circuit, knew where the loos were, where the carpark was, knew where the girls were, he knew where everything was. He knew where the sports place was, and I think even modern teams, which spend a lot of money, miss out on that. They don't spend enough time on that.

I think the main point was that James was totally orientated and relaxed in Japan and with Japan, so when the other teams turned up he was the local boy. It was very much the right thing to do.

There was a sports hall just across the road from the hotel, which James frequented. He and I went there and swam. He played squash and the first day he played the incumbent professional and beat him, so the next day they got a heavy hitter and he beat him, so they got the hero of Tokyo and he beat him, so then they got the hero of Japan and he beat him. More and more people came. In the end they had a glass court with television and James still thrashed them, much to their chagrin.

So he was playing squash, and the hotel was a

Unhappy Canada, for many reasons (LAT Photographic).

stopover for British Airways and KLM and Air France, and every morning he was able to bounce down to breakfast and there was a fresh bevy of females. He'd bounce up to them, as he did, and say 'hello, I'm James Hunt.' They'd say 'oh, we know who you are' and off he went. He was keeping himself pretty fit.

It was like a holiday. We had very little Press around and the Japanese hadn't realised he was there, I guess. The Brits didn't go out until just before the race so we were in a little vacuum of our own.

There were all these rumours that the track was breaking up and, because we had some time off, we made wire grilles to cover every orifice on the car, the air intakes, the radiators, the brake ducts, and we put these on all three cars. Niki used to spend more time in our pit than he did in the Ferrari one. He came down on race morning to see us and there were the cars with all these grilles on, so he ran back up to Ferrari and told them and said they had to do this. They spent the whole morning, from six until whenever practice started, running round Japan trying to find gauze and putting it all over their intakes. Meanwhile we took them all off our cars because the track wasn't breaking up.

Lauda came to the McLaren pit, saw this and said a very naughty word.

We said 'what's wrong Niki, what's the matter?'

Lauda said the very naughty word again.

We used to try and play with him psychologically all the time, quite successfully.

Race day at Fuji was drowned by teeming rain and mist, the race was delayed and almost postponed. Andretti had pole from Hunt, Lauda on the second row. Lauda did a warm-up lap and was frightened. Hunt was always in that state before a race, as we have repeatedly seen.

TEDDY MAYER

He was always frightened of a race car and as you probably know he was physically ill before the start of a great many races. They were more dangerous in those days than they are now and James was acutely aware of that. I think he drove right on the ragged edge.

MARIO ANDRETTI

We started the race in a deluge. I mean, I could not believe they would put us into that peril because there were rivers all over the place. The most dangerous part was down the long straightaway – there were so many puddles. I'm on pole, so obviously I'm the one that has to find the proper way, and the first lap I thought I was going to lose it three times on the straightaway, it was aquaplaning so bad. Then I'm looking to the right and I see some little Japanese – one of the guest drivers – way down to the right. The straightaway was really, really wide, maybe 70 feet at least, maybe more. This Japanese driver was flying so I guess he'd found a drier spot, so next lap I did that. Then all of a sudden I got passed by Hans Stuck and I figured *well, good luck, Hans* and two laps later he was hanging from the trees.

ALASTAIR CALDWELL

One of my strongest memories is that Hunt wouldn't drive [properly!] into the wet at Fuji, amazingly enough. Refused and totally ignored instructions how to drive in the wet. It sounds stupid, but that's one of my strongest.

When the race started it was wet ...

Lauda covered two laps and decided the conditions were too dangerous. He got out of the car, changed and drove off for Tokyo and the airport.

EMERSON FITTIPALDI

For myself, for Niki Lauda there was too much water, it was impossible. Too much aquaplaning, zero visibility, too dangerous.

So what do you think about James who kept on?

That day he was very brave but I think they had a special navigation system on his car! And he survived the race. It was like going to the casino and maybe you get a lucky number, maybe you don't.

In some ways it's braver to stop than continue.

It depends!

ALASTAIR CALDWELL

But it immediately started to dry, as it does, and we knew from years of experience that you could make the tyres last a lot longer if you drove in the wet bits on the straight. That cooled the tyres. We had a board which was printed and it said COOL TYRES. It wasn't hand written, it was a signboard, and we immediately showed this to James and he ignored it, drove on the dry line. We showed it to him lap after lap and in the end it was the only thing we were showing him. We didn't show him anything else.

We put out an arrow which means *you can come in* – we put that on the board straight away, so right from the start of the race he was being told that we expected him to come in at any time. It was a simple system. If we put IN on the board that was compulsory, the driver had to come in, but if we put an arrow on the board which pointed to the pits that meant *if you feel like it, we're ready.* We had that arrow up from lap one.

Then we got really agitated and pointed at the board's COOL TYRES, jumped up and down, pointed at the board

Fuji 1976, and a man alone chasing his destiny (LAT Photographic).

again. Jochen Mass read it the first time and immediately started to drive in the wet – and, because we were holding it up for half an hour, Andretti [in the Lotus] saw it, drove in the wet, and everybody else in the race could see our sign. Other teams started to make up their own and showed it to their drivers. Tyrrell came and tried to borrow it!

MARIO ANDRETTI

Well, I knew what I had to do. I knew that the only chance to have the tyres last the distance was to look for wet bits and I tried to do that even in the straight line because that would cool the tyre down – you get so much temperature in the wet tyre that it rolls right off.

ALASTAIR CALDWELL

But James resolutely refused to drive in the wet. Why? God knows. I never asked him, never bothered. So he wore the tyres through to the air, and then boom, he had two flat tyres and he had to stop and we had to change the tyres.

A life in headlines, front pages and back now.

GRAND PRIX

KING JAMES BEATS THE RAIN

Lauda abdicates on lap two: I just couldn't see

Dassu turns in master show

The sweetest in a long line of British wins

Budget Loan Plan

Daily Mail

EXCLUSIVE: The new world No. One's own story of that race

I SHOULDN'T BE CHAMPION —by James Hunt

Poulson: MP asks Jim for help

ANOTHER CHANCE TO WIN A CAR

The stop went well enough because in those days we didn't practise much and we were only allowed five men to change the wheels instead of 40! It was complicated by the fact that the guy had two flat tyres and we didn't practise on a car with two flat tyres, only one. We'd practised with one flat front and one flat rear but never both. Because it had two, the jack on the front wouldn't work – couldn't get it under. So I had to help lift the car up on to the jack, physically lifted it because I was the one that stopped the car. I gave the mechanic on the left front wheel a hand to lift the car on to the jack and he changed the wheel. I don't know how long it took us: maybe ten seconds, 15 seconds, whatever, and off James went – but of course, with the stopping and starting, and the huge long pit road in Japan, he came out, I think, eighth. We thought *that's the Championship gone.*

By sheer chance – because other people failed – we managed to win the World Championship. Had he done what he was told he could have won the race and the Championship. Andretti was right behind James [from laps 6 to 15] and could see the sign, he started to obey the instructions and he finished the race on his original tyres, won it – because he did what he was told, not by Lotus but by us!

That was my lasting impression of James's moronic behaviour.

Was he frightened by the wet?

I don't think he was frightened. No, no, I don't think so. In a straight line there's no problem if you drive straight. The Japanese guy that was going to win the race was on Dunlops [Kazuyoshi Hoshino in a Tyrrell]. He was quicker than anybody else by a mile. He was soaring through the field and he was driving on the wet side as well, going through all the puddles where necessary, and Mass of course did the same and was going to be an easy winner but he just fell off the road [he was in second place behind Hunt on lap 35 when he went off].

People don't remember this, but we were running 1–2 in the race, Mass close behind James and with plenty of tyre left because he had run in the wet right from the start. Unfortunately he just got bored and fell off. Actually in the end that was fortunate for us because if he'd kept going we'd have had the nasty business of telling him to stop and maybe from a long way up the road – although he would have, because he was a good boy and he wanted to keep his job.

The fact remains that James didn't do that and made it so much more difficult for everybody, then ranted and raved in print and in newspapers about how stupid we were because we never stopped him to change the tyres – but of course we could never stop him, change tyres and win the World Championship because we were never that far ahead.

We didn't do the right thing, we did the *only* thing: the only thing we could do was what we did. There was no way we could judge the tyre wear from the pits, there was no way we could tell him when to stop. James was the only one who knew what state his tyres were in. And we could never stop the car and win the World Championship, never in the race could we do that, because we were never that far ahead.

MARIO ANDRETTI

In those days we didn't have radios so you had to rely on pit signs and all that. I'm not even sure he knew that Niki had pulled in. I was just leading and of course the track was drying quickly but James was not making any ground on me. I kept trying to save my tyres, looking for as much wet as possible: there was a long right-hand corner leading on to the front straightaway and that was grinding my left front away tremendously. The tyre was really knackered.

ALASTAIR CALDWELL

James had Andretti & Co. all there and if he stopped he was going to be eighth or ninth – and when he did stop he was eighth – but someone stopped, someone spun, there was a whole chaos going on. However, when James went out of the pits *he was not going to be World Champion.*

MARIO ANDRETTI

In the end it was a tactical race, a survival thing. Obviously you are never going to know how it would have finished had he not stopped for tyres. Fortunately I kept it on the tarmac and then I found myself leading. It had started drying and you thought *how in the world are we going to get to the end here without changing tyres?* He made a tremendous charge and everybody else was limping about with their tyres almost shredded and he had fresh slicks. He'd have needed three or four laps more to take the lead so we were fortunate in the sense that it worked out perfectly for us.

ALASTAIR CALDWELL

Funnily enough, we gave James his exact position on the board each lap: P8, then we gave him P7, P5 and on the last lap we gave him P3 – actually on the board. Then when he stopped he did all this ranting and raving about what his position was, but on the final lap he'd been given P3, and that was all that was given on the board. He *still* came into the pits and jumped up and down like a big girl's blouse.

He did behave very badly in Japan in the race. Up until the race he had been great.

Japan, 24 October. Pole, Andretti, podium, Andretti, Depailler, Hunt. Hunt 69, Lauda 68.

MAX MOSLEY

Later on the day he won the World Championship there wasn't anywhere much to celebrate, just a very brightly-lit restaurant in a rather awful hotel. We'd all had quite a lot to drink and a few of us were left alone in the restaurant after the staff went home. Every few minutes the telephone would ring, whereupon James would pick it up and say *'Mushi mushi'* (Japanese for 'hello'). The person on the other end would then say quite a lot in Japanese and when they stopped James would say *'Hai hai'* (Japanese for 'yes'), whereupon there would be another flow of Japanese. This went on for a very long time, because on each occasion the person at the other end was too polite to simply put the phone down. James was completely helpless with laughter and so were the rest of us. We were all rather drunk.

SIMON TAYLOR

I was in Japan when we won the Championship and I remember how it was such a tremendous relief and then the partying really did begin, and it continued on the plane going back. That was really when James's reputation as being this terrific party-going man happened. I think it was such a relief to him, it was so important to him to win the Championship. He had had to screw himself up to such an extraordinary pitch to do it that the relief and release was just immense.

J. R. RICHARDSON

We watched it in the broadcasting studios, but I can't remember whether it was at the BBC or ITV [both covered the race]. Oh God I was in awful shape. I think it started at four o'clock in the morning. Mum was up there and Wallis and myself and a few of us. It was the most exciting morning of my life. It was just unbelievable. Nobody had any idea what was happening.

Mrs. Hunt as usual went pale but then he came through in the lead – if you remember, the end of the first lap was the first time anybody saw a car because there was so much spray, and he comes through and he's clear. Then everything lightened up and then the tension started because the weather got worse and then started to dry out and the tyres started to shred. Brambilla did lead, didn't he [and spun off as he drew alongside Hunt and tried to draw away from Hunt]? Oh, wow.

His parents took it fantastically. We went to the Carlton Towers and we had a big champagne breakfast and got pissed again, all of us – a dozen. It was absolutely wonderful.

NICK BRITTAN

The man who had made the not unreasonable deduction circa 1970 that Master James Hunt would never make the grade as a racing driver as long as he had – in the time-honoured phrase – a hole in his arse ...

I was very much doing the rounds of the Grand Prix circuit in 1976 and, about a week after Japan, Marlboro threw a sort of dinner party in London for about 20 people to come and celebrate James's achievement. I was on the guest list. So there were these 20 people standing in the drinks room, pre-dinner, and James came wandering over to me. He said 'hello, Nick.' I said 'well done, James, you cracked it.' James bent over and said, about ten decibels loud, 'Nick, look, I've still got a hole in my arse ...'

Everybody looked and nobody understood. I said 'OK, point taken, World Champion.'

EOIN YOUNG

Motorsport writer

Despite the fact that James was driving a McLaren in 1976, I had been bitten by the generation gap and regarded his off-track indolence as a disservice to the sport. No class. Or perhaps deliberately inverted class. He got a charge out of outraging the old guard.

I had been with Bruce when we started the McLaren team and I didn't think James and his public school behaviour would have found favour with Bruce.

It was the Sunday lunchtime after the Japanese GP in '76 and James was champ. The phone rang at home in East Horsley and a chap said he was a book publisher, he had James Hunt in his office and he wanted to know if I would write a book with James. I said I wouldn't. He wanted to know why. I told him I thought writing books was a pain in the bum, there was no money to be made ... and, besides, I didn't like James Hunt. He said perhaps he could do something about the money.

I can't remember the figure he named – maybe £3,500 pounds, and in 1976 that looked like a whole lot of money to me. He said I had eight weeks to write the book. I suggested he call back in an hour while I discussed it with my wife, Sandra. She said 'go for it' because we could use the money. The publisher phoned back and I said there wasn't enough money. He upped it to five grand (I think) and I said 'that's fine ...'

Minor/major problem was that James was at his Marbella home now and I had to stay at the Marbella Club ... bugger. We taped during the morning, in the afternoon I transcribed, and wrote the manuscript into the early evening. Next morning he read the manuscript and we spent the rest of the morning taping. And so it went. He wanted to do it well and I was warming to him. There was no requirement for him to misbehave.

I decided that if I could find someone to transcribe the tape I would be saving a good slab of time each day so James arranged for an English secretary girlfriend to take the tape. I told her to type it EXACTLY as James said it ... not what she thought he was talking about. Hours later I hadn't had the tape back so I phoned her. She was in tears. She said she was only a page into the transcript because James never finished a sentence. I had been used to taping with Bruce McLaren and Denny Hulme and I automatically ended sentences for them because I knew what they meant to say.

Anyway, the book was finished and the manuscript delivered to the publisher in seven days. Then David Benson's book appeared,[5] the publisher panicked at the thought of going head to head, book to book, with the *Daily Express* – which wasn't a problem for me as I'd been paid in full.

Months later Peter Hunt, James's brother and manager, was on the phone asking for three more chapters – a chapter each on the Argentine and Brazilian and a chapter on James's early years. I said that wasn't a problem – but it would be £1,500 a chapter. Peter was appalled.

I had signed a contract to say that I would deliver the completed manuscript to publisher's approval ... and now there was a new publisher. I suggested if he could find a copy of the contract with my signature on it, I would do the chapters for nothing. I could hear papers shuffling as he sifted for a copy of the contract, so I told him that I'd written the book so quickly that my solicitor was still going through the contract and, since I'd been paid, we never bothered signing the contract.

Peter tried another track and pointed out that two of the chapters were only a matter of sitting around the hotel pools in South America for an hour after each race. I said 'Peter, has it ever occurred to you that I don't want to spend an hour after each race with your brother?' That was pretty much the end of it. David Hodges completed the book.

JOHN WEBB

Later that year we ran a special 'Tribute to James' day at Brands Hatch, where we put on various demonstrations but the whole day was themed on James. That was an occasion where he was really abusive to Brands Hatch staff and caused an awful lot of problems. I remember that, although it was all in his honour, he ended up eating his lunch in the kitchen and Angela can tell you why.

ANGELA WEBB

We had the Grovewood Suite as our main hospitality area. He had invited certain numbers of guests and I exploded: they were actually passing tickets out of the window to more and more people. Eventually I think it was Hot Pants's sister appeared at the door and she didn't have a ticket and she screamed at her sister 'for God's sake get me in here.' I said to Vic, the doorman, 'no more.' James saw the commotion, came over and grabbed Vic by the scruff of the neck, shook him like a dog and said 'let her in you ******* man.' Vic said 'I'm under instructions from Mrs. Webb not to let anybody else in.' I said 'Vic, let her in' – because I thought James was going to hit him.

Anyway, James then said 'is there anywhere quiet I can have my lunch?' I said 'yes, you'd better go down to the kitchen.' As you can imagine there was a massive crowd of fans outside the Grovewood Suite. So he was having his lunch in the kitchen and he said 'at least the pigs outside are better behaved than the pigs inside.' I said 'and who's bloody fault was that? And before you go, James, you apologise to my doorman. I won't have that behaviour.' He did actually do so.

Welcome home, hero, from mum Sue (Getty Images).

And he was so scruffy. I think it was probably the image he wanted to portray. I remember him turning up at my office once at Brands and his hair was dirty, it hadn't been brushed, he had a dirty tee-shirt on and dirty jeans. And he asked me where the Brands Hatch Place Hotel was located because he was the guest of honour. I said 'James, you cannot go to that hotel looking like this. You are insulting everybody.'

Because Lauda missed the Austrian and Dutch GPs while recovering from his horrific accident at the Nürburgring, some critics argued that Hunt's 1976 Championship is forever devalued. Here are some reflections on that, and on Hunt the driver.

NIKI LAUDA

I liked him. I had known him for years and always liked him. Our relationship was based on a mutual respect which had been built up over the previous four years. He had charisma and that's what's lacking today. He would not have allowed these people to tell him what to do or how to behave. I was always very disciplined in my life and he had no rules at all! That's why we got on so well – we were so opposite. In 1976 we stayed close regardless of what was happening and, in the end, if I could not win the Championship, I wanted him to have it. I tell you, he always drove on the limit.

JOHN WEBB

I wouldn't say as a Formula 1 driver I regarded him as brilliant. The fact that he became World Champion was, I think, more luck than ability. I wouldn't have rated him No.1 in that particular year – it was very clearly Niki Lauda.

He wasn't one of the greats, he wasn't a Jim Clark and he didn't have the charisma of Graham Hill, yet he had, a bit like Mansell – who could also be difficult – a tremendous crowd following. They both had guts, they were both fighters, oh yes.

He drank heavily and he was a drug addict, as you know. That goes some way to explaining it but it still made life embarrassing for people like us who were fighting hard in those days, not only to sell motor racing to the public but to sponsors and TV. Whilst he was courageous on the track, off track he did a lot of harm. I can remember one occasion when he had to receive an award from royalty – I think it was the Tarmac Award – and he turned up absolutely filthy. It made life difficult for people like us in motor racing, not just me.

His brother Peter, who was his manager, was a very able accountant and he did absolute wonders for James. I had a very high regard for Peter and he was most certainly the architect for most of James's career.

ALASTAIR CALDWELL

Winning Championships is all about finishing races, not being quick. James had lots of talent, James was quick. So why did he only win one? We wandered off. I'm so big-egoed that I'd say I was promoted to a position where I was incompetent. Teddy wanted to run the race team. I had run the Grand Prix team and Teddy had been between Indy and CanAm. I was given an office upstairs, a shirt and tie, didn't do what I used to do and the race team didn't do so well.

James's problem was that he wasn't the complete racing driver. He was useless at testing but he didn't want to admit that. He knew what he was meant to do, he knew what Niki & Co. did, so he thought he should be part of that.

He knew all the speak, he knew all the bullshit in conversation – because he was a good bullshitter – so he knew all the ways to talk to Teddy and the sponsors or whatever, but in fact he was useless at testing, didn't like it, got bored by it and wanted to go home all the time. We should have done that: let him go off and play, and got a test driver. We could have afforded that, we could have afforded anything.

BRIAN JONES

I knew James reasonably but I didn't know him well. I'm not sure anybody did. He was in a sense autocratic but I admired him because he always called it the way he saw it. There was no bullshit. You always got his point of view. He didn't dress it up for you in the same way that he didn't dress up for you. I remember going to the Tarmac Award, which was a big do at the Grosvenor House or somewhere like that. Everybody was there in black tie and in comes James wearing his famous tee-shirt and ragged jeans and trainers. People were absolutely horrified –

but you had to put up with it because James Hunt was the star.

He wouldn't tug his forelock to that sort of authority. He had supreme confidence in himself. It was a form of arrogance in a way, I would guess, but he did have supreme confidence in himself. He'd got a good background, he'd been well educated and all the rest of it, so the formalities didn't hold any terrors for him. As far as he was concerned *look, I don't do this dressing up bit. I'll come comfortable.*

He was always prepared to have an interview, unless it was inconvenient, and then he'd tell you to *eff off*. It went one way or the other. I think one of the advantages that I had was being recognised as the Voice of Brands. Over the years I found it opened doors because I see all these guys on their way up when they need help, when they need recognition, when they always want you to talk about their sponsors and I can do that. You tend to lose sight of them when they get to the top but they always recognise you, they always know you, they are always prepared to talk to you. That has been a big advantage. It was the same with Ayrton Senna and most of the Grand Prix drivers who've been through British Formula 3 and that sort of thing.

James was a bit Graham Hill-ish. He was brave, there was no question that he was brave, but I don't think he was a natural talent. He really had to work at it but it was a passion and therefore he was prepared to make the commitment.

I've always thought, and I frequently say, that anyone who actually becomes World Champion deserves to be World Champion because you may have the best car, you may have the best deal, you may have had an awful lot of luck, but you've got to be there. And James did it. You can talk about all Lauda's problems and so on but none the less, James Hunt was there to capitalise. That's what racing drivers do and I don't believe there's ever been a driver who's made it to the top and who has not had an enormous dose of good fortune.

If you think about those who were denied, and in theory had a lot more talent, it wouldn't take long to reel them off, people like Chris Amon, Peterson, Regga, Carlos Reutemann. I mean, there are *so* many. The gods have to smile on you, but I think James deserved his World Championship even though he did ride his luck a lot of the time. What else should he do?

Nobody flukes that one.

It's not one year or one formula, it's a long hard bloody sweat from the beginning, and the beginning starts at the bottom end of the sport. For James it started at a racing school, it started in a Mini, trekking all over Europe – that's where the graft comes in. Was it a stroke of good fortune that he happened upon Hesketh at just the right moment? Or were they made for each other? But remember how much hard work he had been through in order to take advantage of that good fortune. For me, it isn't sufficient to think just of Formula 1 – there is a whole story rather than half a story.

CHRIS WITTY

You've always got to be in the right time in the right car – Jacques Villeneuve is a prime example, because [after Williams] he was in the wrong car and the wrong time and not getting anywhere. To a degree Damon as well. So I think James had in Harvey a clever guy who gave him a decent car, the 308 Hesketh, and then McLaren were one of the front-running teams, and if you are going for a World Championship you've only really got to pedal the thing round. That's not demeaning him in any respect. He was a brave bastard: give him credit. Even though he frightened himself he was at the same time brave. He was actually quite a complex person underneath it all. Much of what we saw was bravado.

ANDY MARRIOTT

He had charisma. He wasn't the greatest World Champion ever but he was one who was loved by so many people. I worked very closely with him and Barry Sheene on a number of promotions and they were very similar characters – well, different but similar in many ways, mainly through sheer force of personality. You're talking here James Dean, Marilyn Monroe, Princess Diana – those sort of iconic looks. James had that, no question about it, and he had the personality. I think at the time Britain was looking for a racer of that nature, who had that public school background. That still mattered to people. There was a little bit of the old World War Two fighter pilot, probably the last driver like that, really. And the country was having a bit of a rough time with the strikes and so on. He was a kind of antidote to all that.

TONY DRON

Once he reached the top, his refusal to comply with formalities such as black tie dress and some of the niceties of polite behaviour were, in my opinion, a reaction to what he saw as a world gone wrong. He was quite conservative, underneath it all, with a deep sense of fair play and a loathing of hypocrisy. His party piece at Wellington, and occasionally later, was his solo rendition of the 'Trumpet Voluntary', as I think it's known. James was able to see things as they really were and adopted his own code accordingly.

BUBBLES HORSLEY

When he left McLaren – he never really hit it off with Teddy Mayer – he had other offers. I think he had Lotus and he had Ferrari. He should have gone to Ferrari, there was no question, but he thought of the politics and everything and he went to Wolf. In my opinion, if he'd gone to Ferrari in '78 he would have won two more World Championships. I am absolutely convinced. He had the speed. I think the problem with James was he made a wrong managerial decision to go to Wolf and that cost him. I know he did have a Ferrari offer because it came up in later discussions with him.

Certain drivers have one Championship in them and when they've done it they think that's it. Did you get the impression James was that?

TEDDY MAYER

Very difficult to say.

JOHN WATSON

Like a lot of people, there was a Jeckyl and Hyde side to James. He became, if you like, the first celebrity Grand Prix driver – what Jim Morrison of the Doors was, or Michael Hutchence of INXS.

He was a rock 'n' roll motor racing celebrity. He took his notoriety out of his sport and put it in the public arena. That's one of the aspects of it. It's like selling your soul, in a sense. In 1976 James had a fantastic car, a really great team and, when Niki had his accident, he was more than 20 points behind. He gave 100% of himself to win that Championship and he drove some outstanding races between the Nürburgring, which he won, and Fuji where he came third.

Having done that he opened what you might call Pandora's Box into which you fell, in the Richard Burton-Elizabeth Taylor cliché, if you like. It is ironic that Richard Burton should end up marrying James's wife. James's marriage was a mistake.

The whole thing took him out of just being a Formula 1 star. Who was World Champion last year [2004]? Michael Schumacher. He never raises his head above the parapet apart from that. Who was the one before Schumacher? God only knows! It was Mika Häkkinen. Those two never, ever became what James became in 1976, but the point I am trying to make is that James took what he had achieved and he ran with it. He did a George Best and moved into the global arena – which other sportsperson has done that?

Once he was there, every thing he did, every move he made was going to be captured, and that was what he sold his soul to do, while 99.9% of World Champions live with their own little world. OK, once in a blue moon you might see someone out at a nightclub but that's about it. There are not many people who are capable of creating something outside of their sport. The whole essence of James's life – what he did when he got married, the way he lived, women queuing up outside the bedroom – was to be the archetypal British hero. And he played up to it, absolutely. Absolutely. The irony was that James became potentially bigger than the sport he came out of.

But look at the opportunities James had *vis à vis* the ones that Jackie Stewart had. Jackie is a non-character compared to James[6], yet Jackie was much more astute and used what he had achieved and pushed that towards his retirement, then being a part of the Ford family, whatever – a very controlled man. James had that opportunity and James could have become infinitely larger in every sense.

JOHN SURTEES

The fact is that he won the World Championship, and no-one who is without some abilities and talent will do that. James was never consistent but put in some superb

The book which Eoin Young didn't want to write.

performances – as his record will show. He was a bit up and down. I think that James was not of the more focused type people. He would be totally the opposite of Michael Schumacher and also myself in things like this.

Partly it was his background. In a way, it hadn't been too tough and there is a question of when, at times, he wanted to be a bit larger than life and got carried away. He did like the high life a bit or at least I'm not so certain James liked it but I think he thought he had to play a part. The real James most of the time never came out. He operated in a circle of people where they expected him to go over the top – whether it be sitting there drinking or whether it be partaking of something. I think it was playing a part. I'm not certain that it gave him satisfaction.

There have been other instances of people like this, and the only times when they really came together was when they sat in a motor car. But when they weren't sitting in a motor car they were lost. It's like a little boy lost in the maze of the world: the moment he got into the car he only had to relate to the car. There is a very interesting thing if you were watching the Grand Prix [Europe, Nürburgring, May 2005]. Ron Dennis said something about a boy in a man's body as an excuse for some of the excesses that Räikkönen was said to be involved in – but it comes together when he gets in the car. Because once you are in that car you are in a little world of your own and I think there are parallels there which you can draw.

You've also got the question of the tensions which are built up in motorsport. We had another example in Mike Hailwood. Now Mike before a race was a total and utter shambles. Half the time, people said Mike was on the town – when Mike won the Championship with us, Formula 2, we had a very good friend act as his minder and went along with him. There was no point in Mike going off early to bed because all he'd do is fret. I think you have a very similar situation relative to James. He had to lose himself before he found himself in a car.

And when he did find himself in the car he was a good, hard driver, no doubt about it. That all comes where you have a situation where it clicked in a way of life and motor racing fitted in. I don't think he was passionately fond of motor racing in the way I and many other people were: go and do it in detail, become totally involved. That wouldn't have been part of his makeup, and it wasn't.

Did he know himself?

Notes

1. The traditional yardstick for measuring a driver's ability is to compare him with his team-mate because, in theory, both have the same equipment. Hunt had no team-mate in 1974 and 1975 and consequently couldn't make a comparison.
2. The *FIA*'s rulebook and handbook. It had yellow covers.
3. *Grand Prix!* by Mike Lang, Haynes, Sparkford.
4. American and long-time senior McLaren executive.
5. A book put together fast after Fuji, which *Daily Express* journalist David Benson covered.
6. This is a harsh judgement. Compared to Hunt almost *everybody* is a non-character.

PURE FEAR?

In 1977 Hunt stayed with McLaren, won three races and finished fifth in the championship. He was, however, more famous than he had ever been and that created all manner of frictions, private and public.

Someone said, touchingly, that despite everything he had a very small circle of friends that he always went back to – and that these friends were not necessarily motor racing people. Everybody contributed.

J. R. RICHARDSON

That is absolutely true. He said something to Norm once – Norm was his brother Pete, who managed him and was otherwise known as Norm. That was due to the *Daily Telegraph* misprinting his name. They printed 'Norman Hunt' and it just stuck forever! So he's now Norm to everybody.

We were down at the Race of Champions and we were trying to get tickets so we could go and watch. Norm was under enormous pressure. We couldn't get any anywhere and James, I know, said to him: 'when I've finished motor racing are these guys still going to be about?' So we duly got our tickets, which indicated where his heart was. He was just a good bloke.

The people who clung to him would be gone.

Exactly. But we liked him for the man he was and he was surely appreciative of that.

TAORMINA RIECK

Former girlfriend

I'm never sure how happy he was in those intermediate years, the Formula 1 years. That wasn't the true James. He was riding along on the tide and he was always pleased to see the old friends – people who weren't there just for the glory of being seen with James Hunt, but there because history went back.

Yeah, yeah, yeah. In 1978 a 'Speedman of the Year' ceremony was held in a Munich disco and Hunt joined the band (Getty Images).

The true James? That's elusive territory and to find him you need to confront many truths. Max Mosley prefaced what follows as 'the story you probably can't tell' and I appreciate his diplomacy – but it should be told as it reflects another aspect of James.

MAX MOSLEY

In Sao Paulo for the Formula 1 race, when he was driving for McLaren, he and I decided to go together to a reception given by one of the sponsors. On the way he suggested we visit a friend of his. We went into a block of flats and up to a very glamorous penthouse on the top floor. James's friend produced a slab of polished marble and carefully measured out on it three lines of white powder. James turned to me and said 'you don't want yours, do you Max?' and I said no, whereupon he had both mine and his and we went on to the party with him in an even better mood than when we first set out.

NIGEL ROEBUCK

F1 journalist, Autosport *magazine*

I didn't get on with him at all when he was driving, I didn't like him much. I suppose my strongest memory of that time is Zandvoort in 1977 when he had a coming together with Mario [Andretti] at the exit of Tarzan.[1] Mario had been all over him, lap after lap after lap, and finally went round the outside of him. They came out of the corner more or less side by side with James still slightly ahead but Mario's front wheels alongside James's cockpit. James really did what Michael Schumacher does a dozen times a year these days – it was just as if Mario wasn't there, he just took his car right out to the edge of the track leaving Mario nowhere to go but off. They touched and, as it turned out, that was the end of the race for both of them.

I went to see James afterwards and I remember him screaming and ranting and raving, so then I went to see Mario, and Mario was every bit as angry but quiet. *He's champion of the world, right? He thinks he's king of the goddamned world.* It was all this sort of stuff.

That was a very vivid thing.

MARIO ANDRETTI

That's the only time he and I had some words, primarily because we took each other out of the lead. He was leading in the race and I'm going for the lead and Tarzan is probably the only high-banked turn on any circuit that we have ever driven in Europe. It was quite inviting to go round the outside because pretty much I didn't have the straight line speed of the McLaren so I couldn't get him clean going into the corner. I had a few tries on the inside and once I baited him to chop me off on the outside and I just took a nice arc on the outside. I was totally alongside of him at the exit and he just ran right over my right front wheel. We both went off and later I said 'what was that all about?' he said 'well, the thing is in Formula 1 you're not expected to pass on the outside.' I said 'well, where I come from you pass wherever you can.'

I thought that was a stupid statement, actually. I'm on the edge of the tarmac at the exit and I cannot give you any more room so I deserve that piece of real estate as much as you do and so you have to drive accordingly. He ignored me, drove right into me and is trying to blame me – because I wasn't supposed to be there. So we definitely had a disagreement there but nevertheless it's just the way things go.

I had him and he didn't accept it.

NIGEL ROEBUCK

After James retired, and particularly when he started coming to the races working for the BBC, I noticed a change. One other thing I'll mention, which impressed me and which had an outcome which is inconceivable now. We really did not get on when he was driving. I didn't like the entourage he had, I thought they were too precious to be true – a bunch of Hooray Henrys and very pleased with themselves, and for no reason at all other than the fact that they knew James Hunt. In the end I thought *I can't be bothered with this.* I stopped going to McLaren to see him because you'd walk into the motorhome and all these grown men would start giggling like schoolboys. *Who's this interloper* sort of thing. It was very like that.

One day I happened to mention this to John Hogan. I said 'I can't be bothered with it any more, Hogie.' He mentioned it to James and James wrote me a letter to say *sorry we've had our problems, I hadn't realised and can we start again?* That was not very long before he retired.

HUGH MACLENNAN

When James joined McLaren I found myself in the States and I've been here ever since. We didn't really stay in touch other than he sent me a long letter – a suicidal letter – from a hotel room in, I think, Melbourne, Australia, after he was champion. I don't know what he was doing there.

It wasn't suicidal – I'm exaggerating, but it was just unloading on me about how he was tired of being so popular. Wherever he went in Australia he was being mobbed.

I think at some point in his life he found he wasn't really sure who his friends were. I think he talked to Ping about it and she said 'for God's sake, James, don't expect the other person always to make an effort. You make an effort.' I think that's what that letter was about: reaching out. He was lonely in the crowd. He was in some bloody hotel room and he was saying *I have no private life.*

When I suddenly realised that he was serious about racing I dug out an old copy of *Motor Sport* with Denis Jenkinson's article about winning the 1955 Mille Miglia – which in my view is the finest piece of motoring journalism ever – and I gave it to him very proudly. I bet you he didn't even read it. An interesting question: why was he in Formula 1 motor racing? I think it was for the wrong reasons, and this is the amazing thing about it. I think he was in it for the money. I think it was in his letter to me – or maybe it was some comment he made to someone even in Formula 3 days: *God, you know this is kind of dangerous. I might get killed.* I remember in Scandinavia having dinner with David Purley and Niki Lauda and James and Sutcliffe – and of course Purley no longer with us, Lauda only just, Williamson no longer with us. So it was dangerous.

JOHN WATSON

I think James drove in a very mercurial rather than a passionate fashion. At Zandvoort Mario was doing what I'd done in '76 going round Tarzan, James running him up the kerb. Mario, who comes from a different background and a different school of motorsport, was of the creed that you give the guy room to work. He stuck his nose around the outside, James just rode him up the kerb and there was a bit of ill feeling about that.

That is a summary, if you like, of what James's racing philosophy was. Mario would race you as well, but the perception of Mario always was, at the end of the day, he'd give you some breathing space. If you're racing on ovals you can't pinch a guy into the wall – if you do you won't last very long. Mario didn't want to kill you: that was his expression of how you raced with someone.

Speaking of crashing and cursing, when I was speaking to Allan McNish for this book he said he'd just been watching an old video.

ALLAN McNISH

Driver

James had a crash with a guy going into the Mirabeau hairpin at Monaco – I think it was Jarier who put him off. James pushed the marshal out of the way because he wouldn't get over the barrier. He waited until Jarier came round and he started shaking his fist. Jarier was still racing! James was actually standing in the middle of the track shaking his fist. He couldn't wait until Jarier got back to the pits to show him how angry he was. He just had to do it straight there and then.

JEAN-PIERRE JARIER

I'm sure it wasn't me, it was somebody else! He didn't come to see me after the race and I saw him the next weekend. We were still very good friends and I didn't get a word about that from himself. I was not involved in that thing at all. From time to time, I remember, we'd have a problem with another driver on the circuit and we'd

Peter Warr, who ran the Wolf team (LAT Photographic).

think it's this one when in fact it turned out to be the team-mate. This happened to me a few times.

At that time we didn't have anti-skid technology and we didn't have automatic gearboxes so everywhere we were making mistakes, always we had problems with the car. For instance, you have somebody behind you just in your gearbox and you miss a gear. The guy nearly hits your back and he's not happy, but it was all the time like that: we had so many incidents in every race, every testing period, everything. It was not like today when nothing happens. It's impossible to miss a gear now and even in the wet in first gear you don't have wheelspin.

VENDETTA?

There was a multiple crash at the start of the 1978 Italian Grand Prix, usually described as young Riccardo Patrese (Arrows) moving over on Hunt's McLaren which made Hunt veer into Peterson's Lotus. Peterson was trapped in his Lotus, the car on fire. Hunt, Regazzoni and a fire marshal managed to get him out.

A chaos of cars lay all across the track and the newly-appointed Formula 1 doctor, Sid Watkins, had no official car. He attempted to get to the crash on foot but the police barred his way.

Watkins therefore went to the medical centre to wait for Peterson to be brought in. Peterson was brought and while Watkins worked on him a photographer squatted down between Watkins' legs to get a picture of Peterson. Watkins kicked the photographer. Peterson died in hospital when bone marrow entered his bloodstream.

SIMON TAYLOR

A time I remember very, very clearly was Monza in 1978. James used to be sick quite often before the races – and that implies a very great degree of emotional tension, which actually underlined his courage, because he was screwing himself up so much to do it.

The race was stopped and James had been involved in trying to get Peterson out of the car. Meanwhile, I thought *Christ* – I was on the radio and I knew I had to go and find out what the hell had happened. I went through the pedestrian tunnel because the radio commentary boxes were at the back of the big grandstand opposite the pits. I managed somehow, in all the mayhem, to get into the pits just as James came in.

I rushed up to him and said 'James, what happened?' He pushed past me as though I wasn't there and hadn't said anything, completely ignored me. I might have been a piece of wood. He was sick all over the back of the pits. Extraordinary.

PETER WARR

Team manager

I suppose I should have been forewarned [about Hunt's mental state about racing] because we had already signed him for Wolf in September of 1978, Ronnie had his accident and James helped get Ronnie out of the car. There was a huge delay for the re-start and a subsequent further delay because of us, funnily enough. Jody Scheckter [in a Wolf] had a problem and went off on the warm-up lap. The race was subsequently started when it was almost dark.

In the three hours that elapsed James, who was still a contracted McLaren driver, spent the entire time in the Wolf mobile home pleading with Harvey Postlethwaite and myself to let him off the contract that he had signed because he really didn't want to be a race driver any more. This should have been a sort of premonition of this incredibly nervous guy that eventually we would have to work with.

There were always doubts over Patrese's culpability and whether Hunt hit the Lotus before Patrese moved over on him and hit him. Hunt vehemently blamed Patrese and continued to do so. Years later Hunt tried for a reconciliation but Patrese was having none of it. What we do know is that, when he became a BBC commentator, Hunt was unsparing in his criticism of Patrese.

MARK WILKIN

BBC producer

After years of being a commentator James discovered the Press Room. He came to me after one race and said 'this is amazing. Do you know they produce lap times for everybody's laps throughout the entire race?' I said 'yes, I've been picking them up for years James.' He said 'apparently there's a place called the Press Room where I can get all this stuff. I shall have to send somebody up there to get it for me, of course.' He said 'you know, this is absolutely fantastic because now I can prove Patrese's useless rather than just tell everybody.' He always had that story that Patrese was really a No.3 driver because he was a No.2 to everybody else and now he was No.2 to somebody who had already been a No.2, therefore he must be a No.3.

JOHN WATSON

What went on behind me I have no idea. What I can tell you is that at the start Ronnie went from the left side of the track at whatever angle across to try and split

Jabouille and Lauda, which therefore opened up a straight run for me down the left-hand side. Thereafter I didn't see any of it and I wasn't aware of it. I don't know where Laffite went, but you had Scheckter and Hunt and Patrese, who appeared to go to the right of Hunt, and then tried to cut in. From what I learnt, you had a pincer situation where four cars were trying to get into the space of one. I suspect none of them wished to concede. Who tipped who or whether Patrese's action was responsible for somebody else having to make a move which then caught Ronnie – as far as I know it was not Patrese.

There was a situation where there was a car coming from left to right and a car coming from right to left and in the middle were Scheckter and Hunt.

I got a clear run down into the first chicane and continued on my way and until I came back out of the Parabolica – flags all over the place – I had no idea. And the Parabolica must have been half a mile from the accident. I wasn't aware of what had occurred until we all came onto the pit straight and were then stopped. I remember Derek Daly walking back because he'd also got involved, as had Brambilla who was seriously injured. Derek Daly was absolutely shell shocked. I think it was probably the biggest fright of his life up to that point. We were taken away. We weren't allowed to go down to the scene of the accident and in a sense didn't really want to because there is a balance between what you want to know and what you need to know. So we all hung around.

Through the course of the year Riccardo had a very quick car. Riccardo at that point in his career had upset some people – he'd upset me – because maybe arrogance on his part, maybe youthful inexperience. I was very friendly with the Arrows team and I talked to Alan Rees about it and he said 'we'll talk to him.' When you are at that age and you get a more senior driver coming to you and telling you to take it easy because you might get hurt you think *bollocks! He's just trying to talk me down.*

I suspect that Patrese was feeling people were picking on him and it was the old guard that was on his case all the time. He seemed to be the immediate trigger of the accident, from the opinion that was being formed at that time. Having said that, we all went to America – Watkins Glen – and the drivers said we are not going to race as long as Patrese is in. That incident, and the loss of Ronnie – who was one of the most popular drivers both inside and outside of the sport – meant we wanted our pound of flesh. That was: Patrese wouldn't be allowed to race in America and I think at one stage we wanted him banned altogether.

James was a character for whom, when he got on his hobbyhorse, everything was either black or white. I don't know whether what James was doing all the way to 1992 was the outcome of what happened in 1978 – it's a hell of a long time, isn't it? James had been a commentator for more than ten years, and Riccardo had raced all the way through that time.

James did have hobbyhorses and James banged on about them. Whether he had revisited 1978 in the 1992 season I don't know because, don't forget, he had already been fairly outspoken about Arnoux as well and de Cesaris. It wasn't just Riccardo. James was emphatically right or he was emphatically wrong, there was nothing in between.

It manifested itself when Riccardo was in by far and away the most competitive car in 1992 and Mansell was doing a job on a different planet in the same car. I don't think James necessarily rated Mansell particularly highly but the car was awesome, there was nothing out there, *nothing,* which compared with it. Remember also that James was wedded to McLaren and wedded to Marlboro in every way possible. That was his virtual sole source of information.

Through the 1980s Riccardo was hardly ever in what I'd call a race-winning car. I had my reasons to think it's James putting the boot in – whether it was directly because of 1978 or just James being James. I think he went on to the point where he had to make a public apology. I can't remember whether it was about Arnoux or Patrese, but it was perceived as personal and certainly at one Grand Prix he did have to make a grovelling apology. He wasn't criticising from a balanced point of view. I think the BBC received many complaints about James's unyielding negativity to Riccardo Patrese who, from the public's point of view, was not perceived in the way that James was portraying him.

JOHN WATSON

In 1977 we had a good race at Silverstone. James didn't give up positions easily, put it that way, particularly if you were racing for the front. I think where he differed from me was that James wasn't what I'd call an enthusiast about motorsport. He loved Formula 1, he loved what he was doing but he only wanted to win.

JOHN BLUNSDEN

One of the symptoms, if you like, of intelligence and thoughtfulness was the fact that he, more than any other driver in my knowledge amongst his contemporaries, was really scared every time he climbed into the cockpit. Now the only reason to be really scared is because he was fully aware of all the vulnerabilities he had as a racing driver. Everybody knew that there were risks but all the others, almost to a man, would say *oh, yes, people shunt but I'm not going to shunt* and switch their minds off. James had the ability to win races but he was very, very conscious of the fact that he might go out and kill himself.

This gave him a dimension that other drivers didn't have, because mentally he was having to drive himself through it. There is no doubt about it: he was fighting demons to a certain extent. One prominent racing driver was quoted quite recently as saying 'any driver who claims that he isn't frightened when he comes on to the starting grid is a liar – a liar to himself, probably.' That's absolutely true. If you're so thick-headed you cannot accept the fact that there is a risk in what you are doing, you really shouldn't be doing it. You are liable to be making mistakes which are going to involve other people *because* you are oblivious to the potential consequences of your actions. You become a very dangerous person and James was not that at all.

He was a fast driver and he was a hard driver in terms of *not* being frightened of wheel-to-wheel battling and so on, notwithstanding his nervousness before the start of a race. Once he was on board he was giving his complete self to the driving of the car, hopefully winning with it, and the other worries were gone. The demons were put

Long Beach, 1979, qualifying on the fourth row. Hunt didn't complete a lap in the race because the Wolf had a drive shaft problem (LAT Photographic).

OLYMPUS
CAMERAS
GOODYEAR
OLYMP
CAMERAS
20
Walter Wolf
Racing
OLYMPUS
OLYMPUS

into the background. If you are driving the car close to its ultimate potential you haven't got time to be thinking about other things, but when you're climbing into the car you've got all the time in the world to be thinking about it. During the Championship year, once it became a possibility, he produced probably the best series of races he ever drove. Having won the World Championship, then he had a pretty thin season afterwards and it became pretty obvious that he wasn't going to win it again. At that stage, having done it, I think the fear factor came back fairly strongly.

The fact that he was thinking in the terms that he was, outside of motor racing, gave a clear indication that he was delighted to have come as far as he had and he was with a very good team and hopefully he could win some more Grands Prix, but he knew there was life beyond that – whereas the Schumachers are prepared to devote every day for the next five years of their lives doing precisely what they were doing those five years before.

In 1978 Hunt drove his final season for McLaren, finishing thirteenth in the championship with 8 points.

PATRICK TAMBAY

Driver

I was his team-mate in 1978. He could have been a rock star, he really could have been a pop star. He didn't have a musical instrument but he was a star in his own right. He had his own mind and his own way of speaking – and he was a very, very fast driver, as you know, very, *very* fast.

He was a wonderful team-mate. It was a bit of a shock for me, a guy new to Formula 1, although I had done half a season in 1977 and I'd been with Clay Regazzoni, who was also a very nice guy, at the Ensign team. James was a very friendly human being, outside of racing a great partner, parties and all that. For a young rookie a bad influence! A very special influence, I should say. He was driving hard but also playing hard: he was enjoying himself hard-hard-hard. He had some priorities.

When he was World Champion in 1976 the McLaren must have been very, very good, while in 1978 it was a bit uncompetitive compared to the opposition. So I think his interest had gone down although his interest in parties was still very high!

Did he take you to the parties?

I tried to avoid that – I tried but I got some influences. It took me a while to recover from those influences.

Did you understand that he was not like all the others, a product of the English class system?

No, no, no, I didn't understand that. I took him as he was – a very outspoken, straightforward, fun, life-loving human racing driver. I think he had the profile of the perfect racing driver at the time. He was his own man, truly his own man. Everybody liked his unorthodox attitude and behaviour. What was funny for him was to show up at parties in jeans and tee-shirt, bare feet, and going to prize-giving in his sneakers and stuff like that.

I thought it was his own choices in his own life. I was having fun but I would not have taken that as an example of a way of life for me but I really and sincerely enjoyed the relationship, he was a very honest racing driver as far as technical feedbacks were concerned, very honest with me and very tutoring.

When he showed up in bare feet, do you think he did this for effect – to create the legend of James Hunt – or do you think he was just like that?

I have no idea! Well, I think he was just like that. You should ask Paddy McNally.[2] We were travelling with Paddy – he was in charge of the drivers. We went on the promotional tour in South America and on promo tours James was very, very difficult to handle. Paddy McNally had a handful of that. For me it was like being a kid at Christmas. *My God, what's happening here?* All the time girls and parties and beer.

He took the official events on the tour seriously, no problem. I have seen some guys not as professional as he was on promotions – he still showed up in tee-shirts and bare feet. But he was not making stupid nonsense when he got there and he was honest with the public.

I don't know if I should say this, but between Argentina and Brazil we had a contest on who would *knock* the most girls. Obviously I lost. He got two and a half average a day! Ask Paddy McNally! I was not averaging that, but obviously when we went to Brazil I shunted the car on every practice session. Tired! You shouldn't say all those things, those things are just for private ears.

But that was the real man.

He loved ladies so much it was unbelievable. I don't know about the half, I don't know where I picked up the half!

What you must have done is take the total of ladies and divided them by the number of days.

Exactly!

It will go in the book, but with affection.

With affection and a lot of respect.

Argentina was on 15 January 1978 and the Brazilian Grand Prix meeting began on Thursday 26 January with an introductory session because Jacarepagua was a new circuit. That's 11 days in between, giving 27 and a half ladies. And just before we leave the subject …

CHRIS WITTY

James wasn't fussy! Patrick would have been a little more choosy – James's view would have been it's the quantity rather than the quality. I know a couple of girls, one being my sister, who spent a session with James! I didn't know until years later when she happened to mention it. And there's a girlfriend of my wife's who'd …

Well, he was a man, but they all were: the Barry Sheenes, the Mike Hailwoods. That was what life was like then. James and Sheene were very close, although from wildly different backgrounds.

Hunt had a black lady friend who had a flat in Earl's Court and was very … accommodating.

There was a sandwich between her, James and the man who shared a flat with him – who was last heard of being held by his ankles from the top of a skyscraper, because he would always get himself into trouble. The lady was fairly overpowering.

I think sex probably was important to James in an obsessive way. There are some guys that have a very, very strong sex drive. In the same way that if a woman has a lot of sex she's called a nymphomaniac, that can apply to a degree to a man.

It was important to him. Whether it was addictive – well, I've never been in a position to have two a day or I'd

The other James Hunt, visiting Great Ormond Street Hospital, London. The young patients, families and staff loved it – and so, evidently, did he (Getty Images).

go blind, so I don't know. I think it was important for his personal ego rather than for what the world thought of him.

And now for something completely different.

NIKI LAUDA

I held my birthday party in Vienna one year and invited James along. At midnight I went home telling James that we both had testing at Paul Ricard the next morning and I would fly us there.

That was at 7am and Hunt arrived with a girl he met the previous evening …

… completely drunk and giggling like a child.

Lauda flew them to Ricard and the testing began, Lauda in the Ferrari, Hunt in the McLaren. Suddenly Lauda heard the dreaded word 'accident' and thought immediately it must be Hunt. Lauda got into a saloon car and …

… drove on to the circuit. I found him slumped in his McLaren at the side of the track. There hadn't been an accident! James had pulled off for a quick nap.[5]

Hunt decided to leave McLaren and join the Wolf team, where he'd partner Keke Rosberg, but before that, at Monza, arguably everything changed. See the VENDETTA box. With Wolf in 1979 he drove in the first seven Grands Prix and then at Monaco he suddenly retired.

PETER WARR

Running the Wolf team

It's a very difficult one for me to give my strongest memory because what one ought to do is think about uplifting, funny, highlight memories of the guy and we didn't have that part. The problem was that we'd known James since the Hesketh days. That was where he certainly laid the platform for his public persona and the image people had of him.

My overall memory of James was: how could a guy who, on the one hand, seemed so genuinely laid back and so irreverent and so outspoken – and, to a lot of people, almost ill-mannered – also be the most nervous racing driver I ever came across in all my life? He used basically to crap himself before the start of any race. There are even stories at McLaren that he was sick in his helmet before the start.

I think that is the most outstanding overall memory I have, the incredible contrast from this happy-go-lucky playboy, the-rules-weren't-made-for-me, where's the nearest thing that hasn't got a skirt on because I don't want to trouble taking the skirt off, to this incredibly nervous guy when he got in the cockpit.

In the end it was quite hard to rationalise all this. I made up my mind that the reason he was like that was because he was too intelligent. What he actually had was a brain, and an intelligence that made him constantly aware of the dangers of what he was involved in – and it was a dangerous era, although not as dangerous as the previous one. It was dangerous enough. In sum, he was one of those guys who saw how dangerous it was and it reacted on him. He was basically too intelligent.

So I find it interesting because if you've got those two pieces of the puzzle put together then I think you can put the rest of the puzzle together – where his other behaviour was also a product of his intelligence. He realised that whilst there were values in family life and so forth, the nonchalant ignoring of conventions was an intelligent thing to do to cultivate the image that he wanted the public to have of him. And that completes the puzzle.

What was unusual was that he had the most out-of-proportion body to leg ratio of any race driver I've ever worked with. He had incredibly long legs, so when he sat in a race car he didn't look as if he was sitting too high in it: his behind to his head was normal or even less than normal. The biggest problem for a race team was trying to fit those bloody legs in. They were enormous. He was outrageously different! When you are designing a race car one of the first things you do is take the standard outline that you have of the driver in a sitting position and say *right, he's got to go more or less there.* You start building the rest of it round him. James was a totally different deal because he had so much more leg to accommodate. He was a good enough driver to warrant making the car specially for him, but it was a considerable contrast with what we'd known before.

Jody [Scheckter] was probably the hardest race driver on brakes we'd ever come across, and the other thing about James as a race driver was that he proved to be one of the easiest. There were small, medium and large brake ducts. What used to be Jody's small brake ducts were James's large ones and we worked on down from there. That was also very revealing – there's more than one way to pedal a car round a track and get a fast time. It suggests you're smoother if you're not using the brakes, and the entry speed to the corner is higher and there isn't quite so much of *I'll rush up here and screech on the brakes, try and sort out the mess and get round the corner.*

Ultimately, in terms of our experience with him as a race driver, we actually had very little because he jacked it in after Monte Carlo. We only had the seven races and that was not long enough to build up any real experience of him. You would think with somebody like James, and the image he had, that you'd have memories of raunchy nights out with indescribable things going on and everybody falling about having had too much to drink – a real riot taking place – and that isn't the memory I have of James at all. Instead it's this incredibly nervous guy.

The riotous, boozy evening is a complete misnomer because the first race we did with him was Argentina. We were staying in the Sheraton in Buenos Aires and we all went down to the lobby to head out to dinner the first night we were there. Outside we turned right towards one of those South American steak houses where you get fantastic grilled meat and James turned left.

'Where are you going, James?'

'I know a place – I'm not paying the price that you guys are paying.'

'Well, can we come along too?'

'Yes, if they can fit you in.'

It was under the arches of the railway station, with sawdust on the floor and hams hanging around the ceiling. We had some of the best grub we've ever had and as much of the local wine as you could pour down your throat for less than a fiver each. That was where James was going because he knew that that was where the best deal was. He wasn't an idiot at all. He was very astute, so I think there was a certain amount of huff and bluff about the public persona.

The astonishing thing was that it wasn't just Monaco. We got the message immediately we were in Argentina: brand new car, we were testing and anytime he was

Two into one does go (Mirrorpix).

anywhere near a race car he was incredibly nervous, particularly during the period immediately getting into it and sitting in it before it went off. What happened when it was running obviously worked well, so the need to concentrate on what he was doing drove these thoughts out of his mind – because he was a very good race driver. You found that hard to reconcile with the quivering lump of whatsit on the grid.

He wasn't averse to being photographed on the top deck of a yacht in the harbour with a topless girl behind him. He liked the odd story going about that he'd tried it on with so-and-so – not really because he fancied her but because he knew it was naughty. I don't think that was the man himself at all. The man himself was a cultured and well educated intelligent guy who'd found a niche that could be filled – in terms of the public image of people like himself – and he cornered the share of the market that no-one else was going to be brassy enough to get into. And there we were.

Harvey Postlethwaite, who designed the Wolf car – and who had designed the Hesketh – died in 1999. He gave me this interview shortly after Hunt's death and although it has appeared before[4] it is so perceptive that it's well worth a second appearance. He began by saying he'd willingly talk about Hunt the racer but was not prepared to talk about the sex, drugs and rock 'n' roll aspect of Hunt's life – although inevitably he did.

HARVEY POSTLETHWAITE

Racing car designer

James became World Champion but in the meantime Hesketh Racing folded up and became Wolf Racing. We built a car for Jody Scheckter and then Jody went to Ferrari and James came to us. Perhaps one of the factors was that I was there [Hunt admired him] and of course money. I think first of all I would have to say that we didn't give James a competitive car. It would be very easy for me as a designer to say that our car was perfect and the driver was an idiot.

The car was barely competitive for a number of reasons, probably because at that stage the team was under-funded. We were struggling to cope and this in the era of ground effects. Against that, and there's no doubt about it, James by that time had a fairly disruptive influence. Since then I have made it a personal maxim never ever to have anything to do with drivers when they are waning, because very often the drivers have basically nothing to gain, only something to lose. They will therefore shoot from the hip at anything and everything around them and it becomes a problem.

I'm not saying that had we put the right driver in we'd have done it, but we'd have had a better chance. The problem wasn't only the team: part of the problem was undoubtedly James. When you have a driver who is close to hysterical it has a terribly unbalancing effect on the whole of the rest of the team, and it wasn't a very pleasant situation for us or for him. My own reaction is that it's best forgotten. I prefer to remember him in the Hesketh days than subsequently.

I've said that James was very thorough and pragmatic and I've said this because, in contrast to that James who I could work with and very much relate to, there was the James of the booze and the after-parties, and the James of a chip on his shoulder. He had it in for a lot of people and for a time I was included in that because I think he saw me as the guy who couldn't give him the car with which he could exit brilliantly from his career – but Formula 1 doesn't pardon anyone.

Those post Championship years when the booze got to him and the women got to him and he had it in for bloody everybody, that wasn't the real James Hunt.

Everybody exits Formula 1 out of the back door, you never exit out of the front. It doesn't happen, even to Mansell, whoever. Everyone exits from the back door because it's that sort of business. One of the nice things is that James probably came the nearest of anybody of exiting through the front because everyone now [after his death] has a good word for him.

KEKE ROSBERG

Driver

My strongest memory? You really want it? It's when he shunted at the start of the Zolder Grand Prix in 1979. I had not pre-qualified and he shunted most races – so he shunted and I was on top of the Marlboro motorhome with John Hogan and the President of Philip Morris. James and Hottie [his girlfriend] came to join the group of the three of us, and by 20 laps later he was so smashed that he threw up on the President's shoes. Hottie was on all fours cleaning them and the President didn't blink an eye.

He was genuinely frightened before the races.

Maybe that's why he threw up. Maybe it had nothing to do with alcohol. I don't know. I never understood how he could have so many beers in the course of so few laps. If he was frightened, let's put it a bit milder and not say he was so smashed, let's say it just all came up because of the situation and now you can understand why the bloke retired when he did. I didn't know he was so scared.

EOIN YOUNG

We're at Zolder for the Belgian GP, lunching with my press mates as part of my media work with the French oil company Elf. A mechanic from the Wolf team appeared and said James wanted a word. I suggested he tell James to come down and join us. The mechanic looked perplexed. He thought I'd better come now. So I did, wondering what I could have written recently that had raised James's ire. James was in the lounge of the Wolf motorhome with the door closed, drawing on a cigarette. He told me that he was going to announce his retirement at Monaco and he wanted me to handle the announcement. He said I was the only person in the paddock he trusted.

I said perhaps if I went out and came in again we could pretend he'd never said that and I'd forget I'd heard it. He insisted. So I said if he was going to retire, Monaco would be the LAST place to do it as his retirement would be a footnote to the race weekend. It should rival the importance of a race.

He asked if I would at least sit in and discuss it with his girlfriend, Jane 'Hot Loins' Birbeck after dinner at his hotel.

Our press gang always dined together at each race and when I announced I was disappearing before the cognac, alarm bells rang and everyone demanded to know where I was going. When I wouldn't tell them, they said they were going to follow me. I feared they would but they didn't. The prospect of James hanging up his hat in the middle of the season was totally unexpected and I was the only one outside James and Hotty who had a clue about it. I was terrified, if truth be known.

We talked about it on the bed in their room and came to the decision that he wouldn't do it at Monaco and I wouldn't be involved (my choice) but I wouldn't tell a soul. I didn't. When it eventually came over the news that James had announced his retirement my wife came in and told me. I was ASTOUNDED. Sort of! I hadn't even told her. I hadn't told anyone.

Soon afterwards the phone rang and it was James. I said I heard he'd retired. He laughed. 'I'm in Barrie Gill's office and he's on the phone in the next room shouting down the phone that he's the first journalist with the news that I've retired ...'

It seemed like too good a story to miss my involvement in, so I asked James if I could write it the way it really happened. He said 'go for it.' So I did. It ran as my gossip diary page in *Autocar* and was syndicated to all my other magazines round the world.

Eventually, when James' hectic family life had been around the block a time or two and settled down, he would come to lunch at The Barley Mow in West Horsley where we regularly met to put Bernie's world to rights and generally have a good laugh. If any of the guests at these lunches had an interesting car I'd usually arrange for them to pose with it outside the pub and have a photograph taken, and after I'd asked James to pose I was embarrassed to realise that he was in his Austin A35 countryman. He thought it was a hoot and we had a team photo of him with the A35 outside the pub.

Hunt's 1979 season: Argentina – electrics; Brazil – steering; South Africa – 1 lap down; USA West – drive-shaft; Spain – brakes; Belgium – crash. At Monaco the drive shaft failed after 5 laps and he stepped out of the car for the final time.

NIGEL ROEBUCK

He disappeared after Monaco '79, just gone. Then, once he started coming to the races working for the BBC and he was a journalist, the entourage had gone. Then, it always seemed to me, the real James emerged. The more time I spent with him in these circumstances the more I liked him. He became very good company and I came to realise as well that he was actually a very kind man.

THE OTHER KIND OF BIRDS

GERALD BINKS

Budgerigar breeder and author

James Hunt was a chauffeur to my father at one time. My father was head of radioactive protection for the western world. To cut to the chase, this young man turned up at my father's place at Sutton, which was part of the Medical Research Council. The head of the workshops came in and said 'I've got a young fellow here, Mr. Binks, who wants a job as long as it's to do with cars.' So my father said 'if you think he's OK, employ him.' He became my father's chauffeur amongst other little jobs.

When my father was unwell he'd send for work to do at home and Hunt would bring the stuff round. He was a very Bohemian type really, always had bare feet. Or he had sandals and socks with holes in them.

When he decided to come back into budgies he got my first book and he was reading it. He was on a yacht, the other drivers were laughing at him but nobody could get him away from it – and that's how he started back.

MICK MAPSTON

Budgerigar breeder

The budgie world was not jokey as far as James was concerned. When he came back in he contacted a canary breeder, my mate, near New Malden because he had known him when he was a boy with budgies. My mate helped him on how to prepare and show birds.

James was a very interesting guy, there was none of the signs of privilege – very down to earth, very realistic, although he had lived this fabulous lifestyle. He was very serious about the budgies.

Is it as glamorous as Monaco in the harbour? Is it hell! I think originally he kept exhibition budgerigars as a boy, when he was 14, 15. Then other varieties of birds came along without feathers and he got into racing and all the rest of it. He returned in, I think, 1985.

We went to a show down in Romsey in Hampshire. The man I was in partnership with and I were driving down and James needed to get some fuel. So I said 'well, Fleet services on the M3 is the easiest place.' He went ahead and we pulled in behind him. As he was filling up my mate said 'we're not going too fast for you, James, are we?' James said 'no, as long as you stay below a hundred I'll be fine.' So he could take a joke.

I think Helen [Dyson, his fiancée] was a bit of a fitness fanatic and James was trying to recapture his youth and his fitness.

At one stage he had 150 birds, something like that, although towards the end he did decide to cut down and use a smaller number of cock birds, with one or two hens. So instead of breeding with pairs he was doing it with a key cock bird and two hens. I think he sold his stud for about ten thousand and that might have been an under evaluation because he was in a position where he had to sell. He never paid a fortune for birds. He made a point, when I first knew him, of not chucking money at it too much. 'I just want to pay a reasonable sum of money to start with.' He did buy a few birds that were a bit more expensive but he didn't really get into the bigger money side of things. He wanted to build the stud himself. He was very keen. He was computerising all the records and he had quite a good eye for a bird. It took him a little while to appreciate the finer points of the bird, feather structure, growth, that sort of thing but he was getting there. He was building a very competitive stud and he didn't want to exploit his celebrity. In budgie circles he wanted to be known as a decent breeder and exhibitor.

I used to work for BT and I worked in the offices at Wimbledon so I was quite handy. He used to phone me and say 'can you pop up?' I'd say 'yes, in my lunch break' and he'd have to think about it. Then he'd say 'yes, of course, you work.' He was slightly removed from reality in that sense. If he wanted to do something he did it. He'd been able to do that all his life.

I think he was quite surprised at the development of the exhibition bird over the period when he stopped doing it and came back. When he'd last had them the birds were a different shape, much smaller, the feather was not as pronounced as it is now – the birds have long and wide feathering – and they are ten and a half inches long now. Before they'd almost been little pet birds. He was quite amazed at how they'd changed.

I was at a show in Weston-super-Mare. He'd taken his birds down the night before but for some reason he wasn't able to get back for the show and so he phoned the show and asked me if I'd pick them up, which I did. I brought them back here. He came the next day to pick the birds up and he was driving an Austin A35 van, a little grey van. He had his two lads, Tom and Freddie, in the back. I said 'James, what are you doing with that? You've a perfectly good Mercedes in your drive.' He said 'well, I've just rebuilt the engine on this and I had 65mph out of it on the A3.' He was as proud as punch. That was a measure of him.

He was just, I think, an ordinary guy with a huge talent. A very complex man, obviously, but nice. We very rarely talked about anything else but birds. He would occasionally talk about motor racing because I'm quite keen on the sport – but that was work and the birds were his hobby.

SARAH LOMAX

If he did something, he'd study to find out all about it, the history of it and how it worked, who else was doing it and how they were doing it. He showed that when he started off in budgies. He did his homework.

He could have held himself up to ridicule, former motor racing World Champion now breeding budgies.

He wouldn't have actually understood what the ridicule was about. He'd look at you, he'd say 'well, why is that ridiculous?' and then carry on and make you feel like you're the ridiculous one for even suggesting it.

DAVE WHITTAKER

Budgerigar expert

If you breed mongrel dogs that's the easiest thing in the world. If you breed pedigree dogs it gets more difficult and breeding birds is very much the same. Some of the bigger exhibition birds are more difficult. It's very absorbing.

GERALD BINKS

The budgie part is an insight into the man. It's an international hobby and it might be dismissed but it's very akin to the dog world in terms of breeding, exhibiting, judging, everything. It's big time. You can pay up to £4,000 for a budgie.

It would be regarded in the motorsport world as an eccentricity, if you think of somebody like Terry Wogan who mildly lampoons it – the budgie in the kitchen, or whatever. That's the public view of it. James was very, very focused.

My first book was called *Best In Show*. There were 30,000 copies floating around so he'd have obtained one quite easily. He'd done it as a child, as a raw beginner or at what is called junior level.

The dedicated budgie breeder (Sipa Press/Rex Features).

There are grades in the hobby: junior, beginner, novice, intermediate, and then champion. They are crucial.

He'd been a junior. He began by being laughed at, so he told me, on a big yacht in Monte Carlo harbour. While the other racing drivers and their wives were pulling his leg and giggling, he had his head stuck into the book. His wife at the time, his second wife, spoke to my wife and said that was absolutely right. But James was totally absorbed with it.

The book is about breeding and exhibiting championship budgerigars.

He came here with his dog Oscar and his wife Sarah. He was learning his trade and the only way you can do that is go round aviaries and see what's what: see how things are done, see what the quality's like, find out which style of bird you like, what's winning and what's not winning and so on. So he was doing the sensible thing – researching. I was one of the research group because I've got one of the biggest aviaries in the country.

DOUG SADLER

Budgerigar breeder

People are all the same to me, I treat everybody the same. He approached me, came down and eventually bought quite a few birds from me. I've been at it a long time and I don't charge a lot of money. Money doesn't interest me with birds, it's a hobby. When he first came he knew a little bit about them and he knew what he was looking for. And he soon learnt. He went to shows.

He used to come here quite often. I found him down to earth and a very nice bloke. I treated him as a friend because he was so friendly and there was no swank at all

James Hunt Budgie sale hits the headlines

IT wouldn't be the first time, of course, that the country's media has picked up on a story which they spotted in CAGE & AVIARY BIRDS but I was rather surprised to see that several daily newspapers gave considerable space to the decision by former world champion racing driver, James Hunt, to sell his stud of exhibition Budgerigars.

The media took a light-hearted approach to the story, but from birdkeeping's point of view we can ill afford to lose anyone, let alone someone as well known as James who is in a position to provide the Fancy with much needed publicity.

Of course, the number of personalities who keep birds is legion – but most do not mix with grass root fanciers, like James and, of course, Geoff Capes.

James, fortunately, will not be disposing of his Parrot "Humbert", which readers may remember hit the headlines when it was chosen to take part in a production of Treasure Island at the Mermaid Theatre in London and then disgraced itself by biting the ear of Frank Windsor, who was playing the part of Long John Silver.

Geoff Capes, who is, of course, one of our leading Budgerigar exhibitors – when other activities, pantomime included, allow – is also into Psittacines. He has two Macaws – both female – called "Hinge" and "Bracket" that mimic his laugh. It seems they are

■ Ruth Madoc has her own collection of birds.

Ruth Madoc, who like Geoff Capes has judged the talking birds at the National Exhibition and is well known for her television appearances, has a large collection of birds. Photographer David Bailey had a large number of Parrots at one time and even Paul McCartney, I understand, was into birds in his younger days.

Other bird lovers? Michael Jackson and Diana Ross are but two top stars who keep birds. Sir John Gielgud is another star who has been tempted to keep

■ James Hunt: birdkeeping has now taken a back seat.

Good breeding results at Marwell Zoo Park

BEST known for its magnificent groups of antelope, deer and other hoofed stock – there are also some interesting birds in the collection at Marwell Zoo Park, in Hampshire.

Species which have bred this year include the attractive Red-lored (or Yellow-cheeked) Amazon, a pair of which

ered a chick – but were astonished to see that instead of having normal green feathers it was a fetching shade of bright yellow – a Lutino.

Not to be outdone, Bill Hall, head keeper at Marwell's North Section reports that a pair of Ostrich, which share a paddock with Grevy's zebra, laid 12 eggs and hatched 11 – which have been reared by their parents.

James Hunt going back to Budgies

AMONG the many visitors at the London and Southern Counties BS club show held at Crawley was former world champion racing driver James Hunt who is in the process of taking up Budgerigar breeding as a hobby again.

James, who grew up in Carshalton, kept Budgies as a lad and it was former L&SCBS official and one time partner of the late Jack Robottom, Frank Dodridge, who kept the young James under his wing in those early days.

Frank persuaded James to visit the show with him despite the fact that other commitments at first seemed likely to prevent James from getting there.

It was only the fact that the show hall is so close to Gatwick which enabled the racing driver – cum-commentator – to put in an appearance at the show on the Saturday before hurriedly flying off to Holland to cover the Dutch Grand Prix the following day.

James is in the pr[illegible] buying a house a [illegible] outside London an[illegible] an aviary for his bi[illegible]

Show organise[illegible] tells me that bo[illegible] and Frank D[illegible] oughly enjoy[illegible] the show. F[illegible] not have b[illegible] keen as [illegible] hibits, [illegible] phere [illegible] many [illegible]

the Department of the Environment for their opinion. They replied as follows –

"While the Department cannot give an authoritative interpretation of the law, this being ultimately a matter for the Courts, it is considered that any such release would be illegal under section 14 of the Act except under authority of a licence issued by the Department."

This letter was signed by D. [illegible]eeming (Department of the Environment, Room 11/02, [illegible]gate House, Houlton [illegible], Bristol BS2 9DJ). The [illegible]nce quoted was WLF [illegible]2.

[illegible] paragraph of the Act [illegible]ffect a very small [illegible]y of aviculturists. But [illegible]ould be aware of the

Numerous overseas fanciers [illegible]tended the show, including two fanciers from Brazil. Gerd Bleicher from Berlin had his first judging engagement in the UK. James Hunt, former world racing driver champion, was also present.

Death of racing champion who loved Budgerigars

I WAS shocked and saddened to hear of the death last Wednesday (June 16) of James Hunt the former world motor racing champion. He did not get to the top with Budgerigars like he did with motor racing, but he was, nevertheless, an ardent competitor who was missed when he sold his stock a few months ago.

Few fanciers will have had the experience of being driven by the former world champion as I was. Going down the A3 to visit Doug Sadler in a five litre Mercedes might not be the same as your actual Williams or McLaren . . . but it was an occasion not to be forgotten.

Living in Wimbledon, James was only a short distance from several London & Southern Counties BS members and was not adverse to popping in for a chat. Unfortunately, the show season clashed with the motor racing season. For this reason James usually had to rely upon other people to get birds to and from shows and because of this the majority of exhibitors did not have an opportunity of getting to know him.

Doug Sadler, to whom James went for stock when he came back into the hobby in 1985 (he first kept them as a lad), reflects that he certainly had the eye for a good bird. Doug recalls that James was usually after those big, Buff feathered Budgerigars which breeders like to retain. He feels James would have eventually got to the top had he stayed in the Fancy and not sold his "beloved Budgerigars", as one newspaper described them, when his company collapsed.

Hunt with veteran breeder Frank Dodridge at a show in 1985, and a life in headlines went on – smaller headlines, now (courtesy of Cage and Aviary Birds).

about him. He'd bring the children down and he also brought his dog down, Oscar. He always came in a Mercedes but he took the wheels off eventually – I think he couldn't afford to put tyres on! He'd walk in the kitchen, make the tea. We'd pop down the road and he'd have egg and chips, stuff like that, in the café.

Hunt, however, was poised to behave as (I assume) budgie breeders don't.

GERALD BINKS

He was taking it very seriously. I ran a big show at the time – I took over the whole of Sandown Park racecourse – and James came. He did very well. He'd started to exhibit as a beginner and was successful at that, graduated to novice and then he showed at the biggest show in the country, the equivalent to Crufts in our terms – the Budgerigar Society Open Championship, which is currently held at Doncaster.

DOUG SADLER

Doncaster? We went out and had a beer together and he was dressed in jeans. He wanted to get into a nightclub and they wouldn't let him in. This was the cause of the trouble. I didn't try to get in – nightclubs are not my scene – but he did. He was a tough boy, I'd have thought.

He had an altercation at the door, a proper altercation.

GERALD BINKS

He came to me on the Sunday morning of the Doncaster show. The show is: arrival on a Friday, judging on a Saturday morning and that goes on until five o'clock the following day. So on the Sunday morning James came up to me and said 'do you think you could do me a favour?' I said 'what's that?' So he said 'do you think you could take my birds home with you and I'll pick them up on Monday afternoon?' So I said 'yes, fine.' Knowing him as I did, I thought it's got to be a woman.

DAVE WHITTAKER

They were presenting all the trophies at the end of the show. They called out 'James Hunt' and there was a round of applause – no James Hunt. They called out 'James Hunt' again and everyone was looking around – no James Hunt. The third call was 'Murray Walker calling James Hunt!' – big laughter, *still* no James Hunt. He never turned up. He'd gone out the night before in Doncaster town and thumped the bouncer at the nightclub.

GERALD BINKS

Well, he came here to my home on the Monday afternoon. Never said a word but subsequently I found out that he was up before the beak on the Monday morning – that was James. When he came here he was terribly hyper, absolutely hyper. He was standing in our kitchen chatting to us but you could see the nerves were strung right out and his eyes were dilating. I think he was on drugs but I have no proof of that whatsoever.

What did I make of him? Here's an intelligent, talented man who has burned himself out and ruined his life. My wife and I more or less agreed on that.

His budgies were in the back garden in an aviary. The quality of the birds he was breeding, his best half a dozen, would be worth a fair amount, around £750 to £1,000 – that would be half a dozen. He rang me one day and said 'I've got to sell up.' He didn't say why. Would I like to buy the stud? If you had a yard full of breeding horses that would become a stud, same with budgies, and if you're buying a stud you're buying the whole she-bang. I said 'I'm not particularly interested, James.' One night James rang up and said 'I've sold the stud.' It went to a chap near Spalding, and what the sum was I don't know.

TONY DRON

A budgie magazine front page once carried the caption 'James Hunt displays his winning green cock' ...

Notes

1. Tarzan was the horseshoe shaped corner at the end of the start-finish straight.
2. Paddy McNally, former journalist and now hugely successful commercial operator in Formula 1.
3. The story originally appeared in the *Mail on Sunday* on 3 July 2005. When I asked Lauda if I could use an extract he said 'yes!' So I have.
4. *James Hunt: Portrait of a Champion* by Christopher Hilton PSL, 1993.

PART THREE

AT PEACE WITH HIMSELF

The hardest part is afterwards, which is why so many one-time megastars linger and so many make ill-fated comebacks. The afterwards – the career peak over, the autograph hunters and flash bulbs and TV cameras gone – can consume less robust beings with its attendant problems, sometimes financial, sometimes of emptiness: the higher you've been, the deeper the drop. Each day makes the memories of the golden days a bit older, and the days go by so fast. By temperament and lifestyle James Hunt was highly unlikely to do a job requiring the discipline of regular hours, and his post-F1 business ventures – a club in Spain, a keep fit emporium in London, a squash venture in Germany – all had the same theme: failure. Hunt also lost money in the Lloyds underwriting debacle. It begged the question, what he would do next? For years there had been dangerous self-indulgence because he'd lived like a pop star and now, in the afterwards, the discipline of teamwork, travel, testing, qualifying and driving were removed. You might, with reason, have feared for him, and many friends did. Then a shrewd man at the BBC had an idea.

Monaco, a natural habitat (LAT Photographic).

THE ARTICULATOR

Somebody once said that timing is everything and on 27 May 1979, as James Hunt stepped out of the Wolf in Monaco – and stepped out of being a Grand Prix driver for ever – his timing was perfect. Whether he knew that is unclear. The BBC coverage of the sport in their programme *Grand Prix* was well established, in its third year, with Murray Walker commentating. Walker, the ultimate enthusiast, was zealous of his domain – and his domain was about to develop, much to Walker's consternation.

JONATHAN MARTIN

BBC Producer, then Head of Sport

We created *Grand Prix* in 1977 after the BBC abandoned motor racing the year before because of Durex.[1] Brian Cargill [Controller of BBC 1] wouldn't have a prophylactic[2] on his screen! There was a remarkable about-turn though when James was in with a chance of winning the championship in Japan and both ITV and the BBC covered it. So the morality went out of the window and they all dived in again.

I was the man who hired James. I wouldn't claim that, when I did, he'd end up being a substantial broadcaster. I couldn't envisage at the time how he would develop and I wouldn't suggest that I had any foresight about it.

He retired from racing unexpectedly. There, suddenly, was the glamour boy of motor racing – long, flowing locks, good looking, charming, very articulate – who'd had a fantastic World Championship success against a different charismatic character in Niki Lauda, who was one of my own sporting heroes – and getting James was a little bit of opportunism, really. I liked his obvious charisma.

I always understood that there were moments to talk to sportsmen and moments when you left them alone if you wanted to earn their respect. You never intervened when they were in their 'office'. During his driving career James was occasionally very abrupt and stand off-ish but even then he was articulate and could put his mind out through his mouth. That wasn't always the case with drivers, and perhaps is even less so now.

He was in the great tradition of motor racing characters like Stirling Moss and Graham Hill. There was something about those generations of motorsport people that enabled them to articulate and communicate. Whenever I'd met James in working mode, he did that.

If you hire a celebrity to do a newspaper column you can help him, but you can't help somebody on the air.

You help him on Monday, the day after the race. As I got to know James a lot more closely, once he was working with us, I found his knowledge of sport and his desire to converse interesting. I used to have quite long conversations with him on the Monday after a race when we'd discuss the broadcast, but I enjoyed them because they were interesting to me just as a sports fan.

There are certain ways you can help him on the air but you can't create articulate broadcasting. What you can do is control it, focus it, you can say one or two things to stop him falling into traps. *Do you realise how many times in a quarter of an hour you have used that phrase?* You can buy a *Roget's Thesaurus,* which some of them bloody need – in fact they need two copies of it, some of them. Their vocabulary is so limited you think *well, just look up magnificent in the dictionary and find seven alternatives.* You wouldn't have to do that with James. He was educated, he had a good command of the language, he knew what he wanted to say and he was able to say it.

Continued on page 116

Getting ready to commentate (LAT Photographic).

PLASTERED

MURRAY WALKER

Our first Grand Prix broadcast together, as opposed to any event, was the 1980 Monaco Grand Prix. Jonathan Martin, the producer – this was before he became Head of Sport – was besotted with James! Anything James wanted, James got!

James turned up with his leg in a plaster cast from his foot to his crutch because he had been trying to do a 360-degree flip on a snowboard. He'd seen somebody else doing it, he was drunk and he tried. He hadn't broken his leg but he tore some ligaments.

So his leg was in a plaster cast, he was wearing his horrible torn jean shorts – not jeans, jean shorts – and barefoot, and by gum his feet smelt. He had a half-drunk bottle of rosé in his hand when he arrived about five minutes before the race began. We were sitting on folding park chairs, you know those wooden and metal slatted chairs which you get at outdoor concerts. We had two of those and a television monitor immediately behind the Armco opposite the pit lane entrance with no cover, just sitting on the pavement.

James puts his plaster cast in my lap ...

JONATHAN MARTIN

... I said 'this is very appropriate, James, because you are always so laid back.' James *had* to lay down, as it were, doing his commentary. 'Now James you're *completely* laid back ...'

MURRAY WALKER

... and we proceed to do the commentary. Half way through he finished the bottle of rosé and, to my absolute horror, Jonathan Martin sent out for another one – didn't take it off him, he sent out for another one.

JONATHAN MARTIN

I can't remember sending out for more rosé, I must say. I believe I read that in Murray's book, and I remember thinking when I read it that that was not a characteristic of mine to get a commentator going. Whatever it was, I think it was just a one-off.

Clearly Hunt didn't regard it as a one-off.

MARK WILKIN

The first Grand Prix I went to [as a BBC producer] was Monaco in '89. It was a surprise. I removed the bottle of red wine from his hand and replaced it with a bottle of water. He didn't notice for the first half of the race. He was that far gone. That's the sad side, but by the end he had sorted himself out.

And here are a couple of retrospectives [in summer 2005] which move in unexpected directions.

JONATHAN MARTIN

I still believe, despite the acclaim – and quite rightly – for Martin Brundle, that James remains one of the original analysts on sports television anywhere. The double act which he and Murray were renowned for, and so many millions enjoyed, *was* original. I was listening idly to the Queens Club tennis the other day when Henman was being beaten. He was a set down and I think the commentary team was Andrew Castle, former tennis player, John Lloyd, former tennis player, and Boris Becker, former tennis player. And at one point Castle said 'what Henman needs is to get angry and start doing a few things. He should break a racket or two.'

I thought *there was a time when the BBC would certainly not have had that on the air – to inspire kids who are watching to act in a violent way.* Funnily enough, at the next change-over Henman deliberately trod on his racket to which John Lloyd said 'ah, that's much better.' You wouldn't have had a Barry Davies, a David Coleman, a Dan Maskell saying that.

I got James to do a few things. Because he had played at Junior Wimbledon I put him into the BBC Wimbledon tennis team, not to commentate but to give an alternative angle of a day at the championships. And we certainly discussed taking him to an Olympics doing a daily James Hunt view on one event. The more I got to know him the more fascinating I found him because he was a fanatical sports fan, not just a motor racing driver talking about motor racing. We went down that road with him and in the end we gave it up because I don't think he really wanted to pay enough attention to it – but he was intrigued by the notion.

Although I can remember some moments when he really spotted what was going on down there on the track, I

Continued overleaf

The new BBC commentary team (cartoon by Julian Kirk).

KIRK.

Continued from previous page
regard him most as a fantastic broadcaster and I regard his counterpoint relationship with Murray the same way.

If somebody asked 'what are your proudest moments?' I'd have to say Red Rum tweaking his ears at Tommy Stack at the Sports Review of the Year[1] and the relationship between Murray and James – because it was full of humour, little bits of venom, it was the original TV sports broadcasting partnership and probably alongside that duo *On The Ball*, Saint and Greavsie, but it came around a bit earlier.

PERRY McCARTHY

Racing driver

Funnily enough, I think that James displayed a characteristic that we see in other World Champions – no matter what one says about his World Championship year. We have seen people like Michael [Schumacher], people like Ayrton [Senna], people like Alain [Prost] and, predominantly, so many things happen with these guys yet they say they are right. Other people might think of them *even you must know you are NOT right* but in their minds they are and you can't move them. I think James was very similar to that. I didn't know him inside out but there were certain elements to him that struck me in that same line, there was an echo of *I'm right*.

It came across in his commentaries. This was not a man who had self-doubts about making judgements. James didn't spare anybody's blushes. The vendetta against Patrese lasted for years – because I think he always blamed him for Ronnie's death, you know, but he would take Rosberg to task big time. I remember one commentary when he said *well, that's just the kind of idiotic thing you expect from Rosberg,* and you thought 'oh Jesus Christ'! This was when Keke was at the top of the game. James would say it and defend it, so he was a great character from that point of view.

Notes

1. For medical reasons jockey Stack, who rode Red Rum 43 times, couldn't get to London but went to the BBC Leeds studio. When Red Rum – a national institution after winning three Grand Nationals – heard Stack's voice on the BBC broadcast, his ears tweaked.

It's a fantastic irony I didn't learn until recently [2005] that when I told Murray I was going to use James in expanding the programme Murray was slightly worried. He says he thought he was about to get the push, but nothing was further from the truth.

Walker assumed that Hunt was replacing him and greeted his appointment with 'fear and resentment'. In fact what Martin was planning had been done for generations in boxing: the commentator to describe the fight, the former boxer to give inter-round summaries.

In broadcasting, there has to be a counterpoint between someone who knows the game as inside out as any journalist can, working with somebody who has been there, done it, knows what it's like and – critically – can communicate it. It's no use having been there and done that if you can't really put into words what it's about.

There are some sportspeople who can cross over. Richie Benaud is one, Peter Alliss is another. The younger generation don't think of Richie as a former cricket captain of Australia, they think of him as a very good broadcaster and journalist. Richie took it extremely seriously, went on BBC courses. Gary Lineker, when he joined the BBC – which was in my time too – got himself down into the dungeons with the video tape and the electronic area and learnt how it happens. James didn't do that, James really didn't want to cross over – although after a year or two he was clearly becoming someone that a lot of people were taking notice of on television, not for what he was up to off the screen.

Occasionally I used to say *James, we are getting really close to the courts here.* That was my task as well, to stop him and the BBC getting involved in legal cases. He certainly called someone a 'mobile chicane' – might have been Patrese, might have been Brambilla – but bear in mind this was him starting broadcasting in the late 1970s and early 1980s.

(A subsequent *Grand Prix* producer, Roger Moody, says: 'One of his favourite expressions was a "mobile chicane" and that was just a wonderful expression. Courts? He wouldn't have given a damn about that.')

The broadcasting world was slower and more discreet then.

I was talking to someone the other day about the Heyshel stadium incident[3] because they were doing a programme. They asked 'why were you so late getting on to it?' I said 'do you realise nobody had a mobile phone in 1985?' I heard about this driving home along the M40. I actually drove into a petrol station, jumped the counter and hijacked a phone in order to ring the office. And the kid who was doing the show gawped at me. And so I think James's frankness in the early 1980s was original in a non-critical era. Most broadcasting was herograms, wasn't it?

Dan Maskell[4] was the epitome of good manners. He would be critical of people but he didn't think it was right to criticise them to millions of people in public when they couldn't answer back. James took the view that these guys are in the sports business but they are also in the entertainments business and 'I am entitled to say whatever I like.' I certainly mentioned the courts to him more than once.

Murray's approach to commentary was to go to a Grand Prix and spend hours and hours and hours walking up and down talking to everybody from the highest to the lowest in every team. He knew everybody's name. I mean, Murray would know not just the name of the bloke who put the bolt on the screw but the bloke who cleaned the bolt that went on the screw. James by contrast went to the McLaren motorhome and had a quiet, gentle glass but got to know tactics, what was going on, whatever.

He would then turn up late. The only other guy I know who loved coming late was David Coleman, because it got his adrenalin going. He loved that adrenalin rush and James, I think, was the same. He would turn up three minutes before – or even when they were already off on the warm-up lap. Murray would be looking round saying 'where's James? Where's James?' I remember one occasion James came in and said 'Murray, have you got a copy of the grid?' – but that created this fantastic chemistry between them.

Murray didn't like him in the early days.

I've read Murray's book[5] and it reflected the man: many, many pages in much, much detail on James and I think probably James had been offhand with Murray in that period when James was a driver, or whatever. But Murray didn't like James's approach to life in general.

James didn't really have anybody he would worry about offending because they were no longer workaday pals. It's like when you move from one role to another. I found when I stopped being a producer and became Head of Sport that, although I was good mates with quite a lot of the commentators, you had to put a bit of distance

Into the 1980s and still Hunt dressed just the way he wanted (David Hayhoe).

between yourself and them. I think James did put some distance between himself and the motor racing world which enabled him to comment on previous colleagues – although I think he was always slightly fond of McLaren!

James definitely liked to be quite remote from it all, turn up in time to do his job.

I have endearing memories of James and it's a strange word to use, endearing, but I was fond of him in a clinically straightforward way! The day he died I went into a slight trance, really. I was in the middle of a meeting and Mark Wilkin burst into my office, barged past the very efficient protection of my assistant and said 'Jonathan, Jonathan, I must speak to you – out of here.' I thought *what the hell's going on here?* He told me and I was absolutely shocked.

My most endearing memory, because it recurred every year, was my contract meeting with James. We contracted James on an annual basis, although if I could have contracted him for longer I certainly would have done. He used to come to my office every year with Peter, who was in a way the antithesis of James. If you met him you'd probably think he was a country solicitor, country accountant or even a librarian: bespectacled, slightly shy, quite diplomatic but very in awe of James.

To start with, when I first employed James, I used Barrie Gill. Barrie looked after him. James retired at Monaco, I rang Barrie and we went on from there, but in the end James used Peter as his agent – and it is always difficult with family. I had an experience where the wife of one of our commentators was handling it and she was calling her husband 'my client', which I found hilarious. Peter would come but James did all the talking.

James, of course, had very, very high aspirations. He thought that he was as valuable in any job as he had been as a motor racing driver. This, he told me later – and Peter told me later, too – was part of the enjoyment he got out of the day. Sometimes we'd start at 10.30 in the morning, chat round the issue, and we'd still be doing it at 2 o'clock, 3 o'clock in the afternoon. He used to like in a way to taunt me: that he was about to do something else, couldn't be bothered, didn't want to do it. He knew all along that the BBC had, as a public service broadcaster, limited finances – as was proved to our cost later when Bernie sold the sport elsewhere [to ITV]. There is always an approximate price for commentators, from extremely good ones to good ones and so on, but it wasn't anywhere near a motor racing salary. Nor is anything else! He knew that full well and we had this charade which went on year after year for hours on end where we just sat and played silly buggers with each. Peter told me later that James used to enjoy it enormously because it was the one chance in the year he would get to turn the tables slightly.

Of course during the day there were all sorts of tangents we'd go down. We'd talk about other sports and other commentators and it was a gossipy, scurrilous kind of day – and James loved that. However I used to find the day sometimes extremely frustrating because I had a lot of other bloody things to do and in the end he was always going to say 'yeah, OK, well, I suppose if that's the best you can do.'

During commentaries you'd have James spotting tyres flat – which is run of the mill these days, because there are so many experts all over the place they can get the information – but James did it from sitting in the commentary box listening and watching and communication. I still think though, to top it all, my lasting memory is those days with him negotiating every year in the great ritual charade. It was tongue-in-cheek and he'd suddenly go a little bit tough and you'd think *hang on, IS he going to turn and walk out the room?* He never did but he was clever enough at it to make me wriggle in my chair and get nervous. I mean, he didn't have anywhere else to go but what he did have was *bollocks to you, I might just not do it at all.* It wasn't that he was going to go to a competitor, it was that he wouldn't be there.

In 1982, when Hunt was well established as a commentator, he married for the second time. Sarah Lomax, then 23, was on holiday in Spain and met him.

SARAH LOMAX

I had no idea who he was, no idea at all. When I was at school I didn't read the newspapers, we weren't allowed newspapers. I followed horse racing – flat racing. My mother was a trainer. He thought it was delightful I didn't know him. He said 'why on earth should you have heard of me?' I was at school when he was racing and he had retired when I met him.

The only strange thing is that I did go to Brands Hatch once – and I had forgotten this – when I was 16. Must have been the British Grand Prix. It shows how disinterested I was that I can't even remember if it was for the race or practice. I went because I fancied one of the boys taking us. My friends said 'that's James Hunt' and I said 'oh, who?' I remember looking at the posters and thinking 'I want him to win, he's good looking.' There was a girl in the same race and the boys went for the girl. Davina Galica. The boys thought 'god!' and I thought 'I'm not going for her.'

They were handing out stickers of James, I took one and stuck it on the back of my cheque book.

When she got back to school she wrote her name next to his and played one of those word games – loves, likes, hates, adores – using the letters of their names. It culminated in I LOVE JAMES HUNT. *It was no more than the sort of thing schoolgirls do, and that's proved by the fact that she forgot him so completely.*

They became the great duet: base/tenor, bad cop/good cop, castigator/conciliator, and just this once they were allowed a microphone each (LAT Photographic).

People in the limelight are so used to having people knowing all about them and I didn't know anything about James. My friends in Spain said 'there's James Hunt' and I said 'give me another clue.' Then I went to live in the States for two or three months and what did impress me was that he came out for weekends. I thought 'now that's quite cool.' He was worried because I had a very long commute to work and he wanted to buy me a present to help me. I was very revved up – I thought a car was coming and he bought me a pushbike! That was part of his wonderful sense of humour. He said 'that will help your bottom.' I said 'cheers!' And I tell you in seven miles to Washington DC there are a lot of hills.

I never projected any thoughts onto where he had been, what he had done, what my life would be like, what it would mean, although when he came to see me in Washington people would recognise him on the street. I remember how embarrassed he was. He'd be stopped and asked for autographs. He hated it. I picked up on his embarrassment. That somehow drew a line over it: I didn't need to project what my life would be because he didn't enjoy – or didn't appear to enjoy – that part of it.

His favourite saying was 'guilty'. When people asked 'are you James Hunt?' he'd say 'guilty'.

Then it was a question of getting married.

I was 23 or 24 and he was 11 years older to the month. He was always a very young man in terms of outlook, young in spirit.

There would be two children, Tom born in 1985 and Freddie in 1987. As many witnesses testify, he was a doting father.

We had a baby coach that we'd bought from our neighbour, I think for a hundred quid. It was a London baby carriage, a massive big pram. It was his pride and joy. He'd push it, and Oscar would be there, and every single day they'd go and feed the Canada ducks on Wimbledon Common.

James was not only competitive, he was completely focused on whatever he did. I mean, reading a story to

DRUNK AS A PARROT

Tony Jardine has spent a lifetime in and around motorsport, as a rally driver, PR man and, these days, one of ITV's Formula 1 team. In the 1980s Murray Walker did the British bike Grand Prix and, if it clashed with a car Grand Prix, the BBC had a vacancy. In August 1985, for the German race at the Nürburgring, they reached for the experienced Barrie Gill but he'd lost his voice. Step forward Master Jardine, substitute for the substitute.

TONY JARDINE

I'd worked with James on lots of 'corporates' [corporate events] and so on, he was such a character and that got us more and more friendly: for example we were round barbequeing with Ronnie Peterson's widow Barbra and Wattie [John Watson], James and the boys, in Maidenhead, things like that. But it's my first-ever commentary for the BBC, subbing for Murray, that I will never forget. You must bear in mind we are in a little hotel in Blankenheim and that I am quaking in my boots. I was in a hell of state the night before. Our Mr. Hunt, being the mischievous chap that he was, decided we'd go out.

Blankenheim is a typical small German country town of some 8,000 inhabitants and, in this context, handily placed about 20km from the Nürburgring. The hotel was typical, too: a goodly country inn with its own restaurant, the whole place slightly dark and narrow inside.

When we'd been at the circuit in the afternoon ...

Hunt: 'Look, tonight we'll go out and do what I normally do, *shine* on a bit.'

Jardine: 'No, no, no, James – I'll be in my room doing the last of my revision.'

Hunt: 'Ah, you don't want to do that. I've got a great plan. We'll have a nice meal, couple of bottles of wine and go down the road. I know where the local campsite is and we're going to let a few guy ropes down and have some fun.'

He knew there'd be *girlies* up there. *I* knew he used to get up to these kinds of pranks. Unfortunately I came down and he caught me. I had to give him a massive swerve and make some excuse and leg it back upstairs to my room. He'd already had a couple of drinks, he was on his way to the campsite and he went off into the night. Next morning ...

Hunt: 'Where were you? It was fantastic.'

Jardine: 'Look, James, let's talk about the commentary.'

Hunt: 'Ah, no, no, no – it was a wonderful night.'

That afternoon Jardine faced his great moment, Hunt alongside him. This is the soundtrack to the BBC coverage.

the children: if he was doing that he was doing that, no question of anything else coming into it. No phone calls, no yapping dog or even a best friend arriving. And when he was cooking it was *that*. I remember it very, very strongly.

The only time I've known adrenaline was out hunting and you don't think about anything else at all. You can't. Imagine that in motor racing: it's got to be the fastest, most dangerous sport. When you're standing in the tunnel at Monte Carlo and if you're having the worst crisis of your life you're going to forget that crisis. He took me into the tunnel and said 'you ought to experience this.' He wanted me to experience it. This is the closest ever you'll get to what it feels like to be in a racing car going at that speed. And as a driver you have to be completely focused.

Anyway, when Mummy was selling her house I went through it for my old junk and found the chequebook and the Brands sticker. I showed it to James and he thought it was hilarious, absolutely hilarious.

I love a spooky story, I love a coincidence story. It was one of those lovely moments in life when you think 'I like that, it feels good.'

People enjoy seeing the negative and forget what the stronger side is. His laugh was him and that's the side I saw most of the time as a family person. His sense of humour was wicked – *wicked*. And I loved it. We were very similar in that way. It was a naughty sense of humour and his naughtiest point with me was over Ron Dennis of McLaren. James was trying to light up a fag in Dennis's car – just James, me and Ron's wife Lisa in it – and Lisa was saying 'no way, James. People do not smoke in Ron's car.' Ron is obsessive about things like that. So with a glint in his eye James ate a McDonalds and chips and then had a fag in the car. It was so childish and naughty and twinkling – I thought it was terrific. If Ron ever found out he'd probably have changed the car.

Commentary, the Nürburgring – green light.
Jardine: Alboreto was seen locking up in the esses through that first part of the corner but they all appear to be safely through at this moment.

Hunt: Yes, that was a puff of blue smoke you saw coming off Alboreto's car, locked his brakes. Teo Fabi, incidentally, was very slow away from pole position, never got the car moving so we'll have to have a look and see where he is. I would guess he's probably dropped down to eighth or ninth place.

Jardine: It's the second gear corner, the Dunlop corner at the far end of the circuit ...

Hunt's voice was perfectly calm and that had a calming effect.

JARDINE

We got through the commentary and though he'd nip out for the odd cigarette in the middle of it he wouldn't let you down. Actually he was great, he was really helpful, and great afterwards too. He said 'it was so different to Murray. I enjoyed it' – then a slap on the back. I looked round with ten minutes left of the race and he's gone, departed the box to miss the traffic or whatever. He was brilliant!

The sign-off for that race night was back at the hotel in Blankenheim. The commentary was behind me, I'd released the pressure and had a few drinks. Well, I was drunk out of my brain talking to the parrot in the front room on my own. The parrot was the only one who would listen. I think Annie Bradshaw put me to bed about three in the morning.

ANN BRADSHAW

Press Relations executive

At about whatever time in the morning, Jardine ended up talking to the bird in the cage *and* the fish tank. It was not a stuffed parrot, it was a real parrot. You know how parrots move their heads to one side – it was doing that as if it was asking *what is going on here?* Even the parrot couldn't believe the state he was in. If the parrot was the only one who would listen to him, well, it was having problems.

I put him to bed. That was amazing because for the first few nights Jardine was so intent on this commentary. He'd come down but he wouldn't drink anything and he'd go straight to bed with his cup of coffee. I used to take a coffee up to him. Then he had the release: it all worked and off we went. He was entitled to.

James was the exact opposite. He was having threesomes in his bedroom. There was him, a girlfriend and another one and they kept asking for ... orange juice.

To tell James he couldn't was the wrong thing to say and I know that from our children. One is similar to him ...

After the divorce Hunt fell on hard times.

TONY DRON

His rusty Austin A35 van gave him pleasure: we both always liked driving low performance cars on the road. He said of that van: 'Round the Wandsworth one-way system, in the wet at night, I can give it everything I ever learnt in racing, carve up the Ferraris, and nobody takes any notice.' Sadly, it failed the MoT because of the rust and he could not afford to repair it. A friend of mine in the trade offered him a very good deal for the work but he just had no money at all at that time.

His transport became a broken down old push-bike (a ladies' model he picked up for nothing) which, because of his strength, used to break up as he pedalled furiously around London. It was regularly welded back together, he told me, by a blacksmith in Putney.

Notes

1. Durex sponsored the Surtees Formula 1 team between 1976 and 1978.
2. A preventative course of action, but particularly in the United States, a condom.
3. The 1985 riot in the Brussells stadium before the match between Liverpool and Juventus, when 38 people died.
4. Maskell had a deep voice, a photographic memory and never expressed strong views. His trademark, when a good shot had been played was, 'oh, I say!'
5. *Unless I'm Very Much Mistaken,* Murray Walker, HarperCollins.

LIGIER

THE SOUND AND THE FURY

Three stories, one from the commentator – Murray Walker – and two from the BBC producers, Roger Moody and Mark Wilkin. Each coped with Hunt in their different ways. I am quoting them verbatim and with the lightest editing. The fact that their words are not all neatly tied up accurately reflects the coping.

MURRAY WALKER

My strongest memory? Crumbs, it should immediately come to the top of your mind. I think probably ... his cheerfulness, bonhomie – which is not what I really expected to say when I started thinking about it.

He was an extremely complex character. I have often reproached myself for being a bit harsh in my outlook towards James when I first knew him but I have talked to a lot of people about it subsequently and they all agree with me that in his early days, indeed right up to the time when he had finished driving, he was an arrogant, self-opinionated so-and-so, and putting up with his Hooray Henryish characteristics was very difficult. But over the years he mellowed considerably.

I have always thought his behaviour in those early days was because, when he was at the height of his driving career, everything was thrown at him – women, money, cars, everything you can think of – as a result of which, in a situation where he was a hyper confident, not to say arrogant, bloke in the first place, all those things were exacerbated.

But if you or I had behaved like that we'd have been fired or thumped or whatever.

Hunt made the transition from the pop idol of Grand Prix racing to become one of its elder statesmen (LAT Photographic).

That's right. James could get away with it because he was James, because they wanted him for something. But again it's always been a theory of mine that when he fell on his hard times after his second marriage, and losing money at Lloyds, a bit of humility actually entered his character – which was most unexpected – and he threw aside the attitude he'd had before. You will remember the days when he used to go into the Media Centre seeking out the knowledge and chatting to people, whereas previously he would never do that

It was years before he discovered there was a Press Centre. 'Why didn't someone tell me before?'

That incidentally is typical of James. Why didn't somebody tell me before, rather than why didn't he take the bloody trouble to find out for himself?

One thing that has always intrigued me is that the tension between you and him was never communicated to the viewers.

Again I have talked to myself many times about why in a situation when I had all these bottled up feelings about this bastard who was trying to nick my knowledge and was too bloody lazy to communicate in the box – that sort of thing – it didn't manifest itself in some way in my commentary or, for that matter, in his. I really don't know the answer. I like to think that I was professional enough that my irritation didn't show. It wasn't my dislike of him, incidentally, because I didn't dislike him. He just irritated me.

I resented the fact that he didn't get stuck into it the way I did – but the fact of the matter is, if you look at it logically, he didn't need to get stuck in the way I did because he had things that more than balanced the equation by virtue of the fact that he'd been there and done that, and the fact that he was an outspoken chap who didn't mind what he said, and by virtue of the fact that he actually knew what he was talking about.

One of the many things that used to irritate me about him, however, was his totally unreasoned attitude to people he didn't like, such as Patrese. He used to sound off about Ken Tyrrell. He had a fixation that some time or other in Jody Scheckter's career when he was with Ken Tyrrell, Ken had sent him out to do something on a set of worn Goodyear tyres and he should never have done this because, in James's opinion, it was dangerous. He used to be totally unreasonable in his attitude towards Ken. Then there was Patrese and Nigel of course – 'a Brummie whinger'. The difference between James and me was that James had the courage – or the temerity, or whatever you like to call it – to say it, whereas I had the diplomacy, or whatever you like to call that, not to say it.

I think I used to resent the fact that James was not a team player in the sense that Martin Brundle is, for instance, and again I should *not* have resented this because it was just a manifestation of the man. But you were always having to make allowances for James, everybody had to defer or accede to his point of view – or have a bloody argument.

I remember on one occasion having a briefing meeting at the Channel 9 in Adelaide and something cropped up about Nigel. James piped up and said 'oh, Murray won't do that, he's a Mansell toady.' I don't think I've ever lost my temper with anybody, or even spoken out against anybody – which perhaps I should have done – but I remember that really cut deep because I didn't regard myself as a Mansell toady. Just because I wasn't outspoken about Mansell, James apparently thought I was.

I don't know how you got through it.

With hindsight I don't either. I was constantly having to adopt an accommodating attitude, although in fact maybe our broadcasts were improved because of mutual imperfections.

You need the professional commentator and the expert who looks at it from a completely different point of view.

Yes, but there are two caveats. One is that the professional racer – or whatever – has also got to be intelligent and able to communicate; and the other is that, in the final analysis, they have to be able to work together even if there's friction. If you can't stand each other, to the extent that you can't even get into the box together, then you are going to be in dire trouble.

There seems no doubt that James did take some of the naughty stuff as well.

I don't know what he took exactly but he certainly did. I was coming back from Paul Ricard in the car with Roger Moody, James and the sound bloke. We were driving along the road from Bandol to wherever we were going and James suddenly said 'ah, I'd like a smoke. Anybody want a smoke?' I remember thinking *this is a bit odd.* What James meant was one of these marijuana things. So James said 'what about you, Murray?' I said 'no thanks, James, I don't smoke.' I really thought he was going to be smoking a cigarette.

Then we came upon a French police road block. They used to stop traffic just because they could and James got in a hell of a lather. He was saying 'wind the windows down, wind the windows down' and he was flapping about with a piece of paper. I suddenly realised what it was that he was up to.

Whatever he was, he was also a lovable, endearing chap and, with the passage of time, I look back on him with great affection, and wish I hadn't had the feelings of irritation and all the rest of it which I quite justifiably had at the time.

One thing struck me, and that was that he was a wonderful father. A week before the Portuguese Grand Prix he used to bring his sons Freddie and Tom as little children to the weird hotel that we stayed at. They had a nanny, and on the race days James was off to the circuit, but he was always most caring and conciliatory and played with them. I thought *well, I really wasn't expecting him to be like that.*

ALAN JENKINS

James was a one-off, completely. I never saw a bad side of him because he'd quietened down a lot when I lived in the New Forest in my Penske days and we became pally.

Kindred spirits. Motorcycle champion Barry Sheene, who was as irreverent as Hunt himself (LAT Photographic).

We got very pally with Murray Walker because he lived not very far away. We saw Murray a bit and we saw how Murray's view of him changed over the years. They became pretty close. At that point I found him one of the easiest guys to be with. I wouldn't say I felt that about all his friends. If you met him in London you thought 'God, who are some of these people?'

ROGER MOODY

BBC producer

I don't think James gave two stuffs about what people thought of him.

I was producer for *Grand Prix*, particularly on site at the racetracks around the world, and the most frustrating thing with James was occasionally asking whether he would ever turn up. I frequently used to say to him 'can you get to the commentary box with Murray nice and early so you can settle in and get into the things?' Murray used to start his commentary and then put his hand over the mike ...

Walker: 'Where is James?'

Moody shrugs shoulders: *no idea*.

Actually we knew he was probably in the Marlboro motorhome having a good time or recovering from the night before when he'd had a good time. So Murray would start the warm-up lap, get half way through and put his hand over the mike again ...

Walker: 'WHERE IS JAMES?'

Moody: 'No idea, Murray, keep on talking.'

So the formation lap had taken place and the last car would be coming to a halt on the grid and the green light would be seconds away. James would saunter in, denim trousers just above the knee, no shoes, fag in hand, blond hair all over the place and he'd say 'OK, let's go, chaps,' and once again I'd be breathing a sigh of relief. That was one of his idiosyncrasies.

The other was that he had had a few drams, either the night before or even before coming up into the commentary box. He used to nod off and let Murray go on – which from a producer's point of view was a bit frustrating – but a sharp dig in the ribs brought him back into the action. He would always slump down in his seat [even when perfectly alert], Murray would stand up. I remember at the French Grand Prix one year we were in a very, very hot box and Murray would be thrashing about like Murray always used to and the sweat would be pouring off him, literally dripping off him, and it would drip on to James. He'd take no notice – probably be asleep, actually.

And there was one famous occasion where we were all waiting for him to turn up and he didn't – Belgium – when he'd obviously had a very good night, and the word came back that he'd got food poisoning. To the best of my knowledge, that was the only time he failed to show.

We always knew, to start with, that Murray thought James would lower the tone really, and not be a perfect foil, but in the end they grew so well together that Murray was completely turned about.

I don't think initially I, as the *Grand Prix* producer, realised that James was going to come to the wicket as much as he did, but all credit to Jonathan Martin for getting him. We'd had some of the previous racing drivers – no names, no pack drill – who didn't want to upset anybody, which got terribly boring. James would say exactly what he thought and, ironically enough as far as I'm aware, not only did the public love him for that but so did motor racing insiders as well. They accepted James for what he was. And if you tackled him about what he'd said, he'd always defend it. All the more shame there aren't more characters like him around today. Martin Brundle does a terrific job – yes, he does – but there will only ever be one James Hunt.

I think James was so insular – no, that's not the right expression – he was so much his own person that he suffered fools very lightly, and it was not always that easy, particularly when you had a working relationship, to get beyond the façade of the man. I don't know how many close friends he had.

Everybody knows that they worked with only one microphone between them but that had become a sort of BBC tradition, not necessarily just for motorsport. The BBC were concerned in those days that commentators would talk across each other if you had two microphones. It's quite a strong discipline not to pick up your own individual mike and talk when someone else is talking – so that evolved from other aspects of BBC sports coverage, it wasn't unique to James and Murray or motor racing as far as I am aware.

Murray wouldn't show if he was dramatically upset. He always used to go to his room and do his research for the following day so if we were out and about – 'look, we're off to a club' – Murray would say 'ah, no, I've got to do some research.' It may be that occasionally he went off a bit earlier to do his research if he was cheesed off with somebody but you'd never really know that. Murray was the gentleman and you could never actually say that James was a gentleman!

He was deeply frustrating, he wasn't a team player, but you couldn't do without him. Towards the end he was definitely calming down and, looking back, James was the most wonderful, likeable chap to work with. He was always very hospitable, he would ask us round to his house in Wimbledon. He and Sarah, my wife and I all got on very well together. I remember Estoril and the Portuguese Grand Prix where he brought the kids down and we were all on the beach and it was a wonderful time ...

MARK WILKIN

A lot of people don't know who he really was: there was a whole heap of Jameses, not just the one side which a lot of people saw: bare-chested, just a pair of shorts and no shoes, walking up the pit lane trying to find the commentary box.

It was a question of trying to manage, really, just trying to make him understand what problems we were trying to deal with. He had a great habit of switching off if the race became dull and he tended to say it: *well, this is dull* – and you can't really say to the viewers 'don't bother watching the rest of it.' I used to spend quite a lot of time talking to him about what we were doing, what we were trying to do, what commentary was about, and how we could make it better. We'd go through and find things he could talk about when he wasn't visually stimulated – he worked very well when he was stimulated by the pictures, and he tended not to bother much when he wasn't.

We had to find strategies for things which were interesting, say, to keep stories back that we had saved up from the conversations we'd had over the weekend rather

Friends of a lifetime. Niki Lauda hammers out his logic, Hunt and Jochen Mass listen (Getty Images).

CHANGING ROOMS

MURRAY WALKER

I remember when the Spanish Grand Prix was at Jerez we used to stay at some sort of holiday camp at Rota [on the coast], near the American army base, and for some reason James's private hotel arrangements foundered. He came storming into the hotel late at night saying to Mark Wilkin 'where is my hotel room?' – where he'd never ever claimed one: charged one but never claimed one. And so we all had to scatter round and move around. Mark said he wanted me to move in with someone and I said 'bugger that! I've got my room. James has fouled up his arrangements. That's his problem.' In the end Mark or whoever it was – the sound man – bunked up together and he got their room. That was typical of James. In that respect he didn't change.

MARK WILKIN

He decided that he didn't like any of the furniture in his hotel room and dragged it all outside into the hall. That was in the rather nice Riviera hotel, in a village on the coast, we stayed during the French Grand Prix for Paul Ricard. It was called something like the Balmoral – it wasn't, but it had a very English name. We always stayed there. It was a fabulous place but it hadn't really seen a lick of paint since the 1930s, and the service was pretty similar as well. They hadn't obviously changed the furniture in the room either, and James decided that he didn't like any of it. So he put the whole lot outside, dragged the mattress back in and slept on that.

Only a very eccentric man would do that and get away with it. That was always the point with James: he could do virtually anything he liked and he always got away with it. For strangers there was the charming smile and the cheeky wink but the people who knew him knew he could do whatever he liked. He had this utter belief that whatever he did he would get away with it, built on a lifetime's experience of doing exactly that.

MURRAY WALKER

Why would he haul bedroom furniture into the corridor? You [the author] are asking the question as a normal, balanced human being. James was neither normal nor balanced in many ways.

than deliver them on the first lap when things were terribly exciting and he had lots of visual stimulation. So we saved those for the dull bits.

I remember the first race we had to stay live with. *Grandstand* would usually stop as soon as they went past the chequered flag and go off somewhere else. The rules changed and we had to stay live for the post-race celebrations, the podium and the champagne spraying and so on.

Wilkin: 'Save your summing-up for after the race rather than do it on the last lap as normal.'

Hunt: 'Well, what will I talk about?'

Wilkin: 'Just say the same things that you usually do.'

Hunt: 'Yes, but I'm usually fired off by the pictures and I won't have any pictures to talk about.'

That was how he worked: the brain was fired up by what he saw and that triggered all the stuff that he came out with, as opposed to being a natural born raconteur who could just tell stories come what may. But he developed quite well and in the end we stayed live at the end of every race. He worked out how to do that. Then I'd point to the screen and say 'talk about the guy that's won' and once he'd got to the end of that he'd go on to number 2, then number 3 and it would go on that way, which was terrific. He was a quick learner because he was a bright guy.

Another side to him. We used to have a nice lunch at the end of the season. We would generally invite everyone involved with the programme internally, but also some of the people who had helped us externally through the course of the year – people who we felt we owed something to. It was quite smart, suits and ties, in town. James always turned up in a pair of shorts having been on his bicycle. He'd greet everyone else – always there ahead of him – with a hasty 'hello', then disappear off into the loo and come out looking immaculate in his suit. When he was in straitened circumstances he cycled everywhere. He discovered cold showers as well, shortly before he died, which he rather enjoyed! He thought this was the latest health kick: having done whatever it was that he was doing, he'd stand under the shower for five minutes with it on full cold, which is probably what finished him off.

I said to him once 'are you taking your girlfriend to Italy?' and he said 'Take a girl to Italy? Are you mad!'

SIMON TAYLOR

Murray had enormous misgivings and Murray was very upset initially but James was so intelligent. He really was the first person, and I think the only person before Martin Brundle, to bring a kind of intelligent, calm perspective. The thing worked so well because, in the true sense of the word, Murray and James were complementary. It was the Yin and Yang. They both did it completely differently.

As you know, they had this ludicrous system where they shared the same microphone, which was the only way Jonathan Martin could find to stop them talking over each other.

I remember the Hungarian Grand Prix in 1986 when it coincided with the motorcycle Grand Prix and Murray wasn't there. The BBC said to me 'don't do the radio, go and do the TV.' I went and did that with James. It was interesting because it was the first time I'd really had to be with James at work since he'd been a Formula 1 driver.

There was again this curious mix: externally, being incredibly laid back and not taking it very seriously – you've heard all the stories of him turning up in the commentary box with a bottle of wine, wearing a filthy pair of frayed shorts and no socks and shoes – and we had to do this daft business of sharing one microphone, *but* what I found great from my point of view was that I was taking my job seriously and he was taking his job seriously too.

I don't think he quite knew at the start how it was going to work, but it did work and at the end he very charmingly said that he'd really enjoyed it and it had gone well, or something like that. Quite clearly it mattered to him, and you had this curious mix of being scruffy and laid back and being professional and wanting to do the job in an intelligent way, which was just like he had been in Formula 1.

Since we've heard Tony Jardine at the start of his race with Hunt, here is Taylor in precisely the same situation:

Commentary, the Hungaroring, 1986

Taylor: We have a red light, 76 laps to go, there is the green. An excellent start by Mansell but it is Senna who has the inside line. Senna leads, Mansell tucked right under his rear wing, Riccardo Patrese going outside of the first corner to go into third place so it's a Williams second and third, then the two Benettons ... but it's Senna who made an absolutely copybook start, Senna leads the queue as they go down the valley, through the tight series of corners ... now the drag up the hill. It's Senna from Mansell, Patrese is up to third, then the two Benettons, then Gerhard Berger who's made a wonderful start, then it's Capelli, behind Capelli is Gugelmin, then Alain Prost who, remember, started well down, but he's nicely placed and he's going to take care in this early lap.

Hunt: Yes, marvellous start from Senna because he got the rear wheels spinning, a little bit slow on traction but he had the revs up on the engine and then as the rear wheels finally bit he was able to outdrag Mansell who also made a superb start – but they can't compete really with the power of the turbo. But look at that, Mansell closing right up on Senna in the twisty section of the track. Prost made a relatively tardy start from seventh place on the grid and is now down in ninth or tenth and that's given him an awful lot of work to do because for Prost and Senna this is a very critical race for the drivers' World Championship. And remember it's only really wins that are going to count. Prost has left himself an awful lot to do.

The cars were now rounding the final corner for the straight and the completion of the lap. You could hear Hunt moderate the tone of his voice as he completed the sentence — as if to indicate: I am winding up and passing back to you.

HELEN DYSON

In his commentaries he used code language! What was it? I'm not telling you! It was in the things he used to say: phrases and words, and they were very funny. I'd be watching at home – and he'd be checking I was watching. We did have a giggle, yes! Murray wouldn't have known.

THE SEDUCTRESS, AND THE MARKS WHICH NEVER WERE

Some stories, they say, are too good to check but this one was far too tempting for that. Moreover it demonstrates the difference between treasured mythology – so necessary in human affairs (pun intended) – and reality. First the mythology, well known to motorsport people of a certain age.

NICK BRITTAN

There was a Dutch magazine laughingly known as a lifestyle magazine. It was very soft porn and had a female feature writer – extremely blonde, extremely tall, extremely big-titted and attractive. Her job was to go and entrap leading sportsmen – tennis players, golfers, whatever – and bonk them, right? Spend the weekend with them, have a romantic dinner. The name of her game was *I bonked with so-and-so, this is the story of how I did it, this is where we went for the weekend – we went to a fashionable resort, or I got laid in his house.* Full chapter and verse, all in Dutch, and at the end of it she scored the person in the same way that they score in ice-skating. She did style and technical merit out of 10 – at the end of her articles would be two scoreboards.

Everybody in the paddock knew about this magazine because the edition before had had some famous football player in it, and anyway it used to get passed around the paddock. People laughed at it. *Look at that footballer, look what he scored.*

James was obviously on her list. At that time James was living in Spain, down just outside Malaga. Jenny and I also had a house there and, coming back, we were sitting on the plane: last man running up the steps is J. Hunt.

He comes wandering down the aisle, there's a spare seat where we are, he sat between me and Jenny. In the course of conversation James says *guess what I've been doing, guess why I'm late? I've just had two glorious days with* – whatever her name was. *She's been road testing me for her latest article. It was absolutely bloody fantastic and I have bonked her brains out.* And so on, blah, blah, blah. *Guaranteed I've got to get two 10s.*

Two weeks later at the next Grand Prix there is the magazine and it's going round the paddock like a bolt of lightning, everybody guffawing. James scored 8 for style and 5 for technical merit. At that time I was writing a column in *Autosport*, which was scurrilous, perhaps. I retold the story of James believing he was going to get two 10s and how ultimately he was devastated to have got an 8 and a 5. The next Grand Prix, James came up to me.

'Nick, where did you get this crap that you've just written about me reckoning I was going to get 10s?'

'James, you were sitting on the aeroplane next to me with Jenny on the other side telling you'd bonked her brains out.'

'Oh, did I? All right, then.'

The magazine was called Nieuwe Revue and the writer was Alissa Morrien. Hunt had had warning because some weeks before, in a piece about her in the News of the World, she announced he was next. As you can see, she wasn't big and she wasn't blonde. This is a condensed version of what happened when she journeyed to Spain. It begins, unromantically, with a jog.

'Shall I show you the rest of the house?' asks James, still out of breath from the run. I nod and ask myself if he will push me on the bed when showing the bedroom but

The Dutch magazine Nieuwe Revue and their 'reporter' Alissa Morrien gave Hunt plenty of warning – relayed by the News of the World (courtesy Nieuwe Revue).

ALISSA'S magazine: rating stars' sexiness

Merroney a naughty boy

By Fiona Macdonald Hull

UTCH magazine reporter Alissa Morrien has been telling er readers all about her nude frolics with leading British V actor Colin Baker.

Alissa, 31, was on an assignment to assess the sexiness of Europe's most attractive men. Next on her list is racing driver James Hunt.

What happened when he went Dutch with Alissa from Amsterdam

She claimed that Colin Baker, who plays the cold, calculating Paul Merroney in The Brothers, said he wanted to make love to her—and she agreed it was a good idea.

But did they?

Alissa reports: "I won't tell any more. It doesn't concern anybody."

The article, with pictures showing Colin and Alissa naked in a sauna bath, appears in Holland's Nieuwe Revu[e].

"Colin was so nice," Alissa tells her 20,000 readers.

"I had just interviewed a Dutch quizmaster in the bath, and Colin wanted to know how he could go one better.

"So I suggested we did the interview in an Amsterdam sauna."

At first Colin was a bit bashful about undressing in the private sauna she hired for the day, said Alissa.

But he soon lost his nervousness after she started to strip off.

Priest

"I'm glad you got undressed first," he told her. "That makes it easier for me."

Then, according to Alissa, Colin confessed: "I was brought up a Catholic and until my teens I wanted to be a priest.

"But that went completely by the board after I discovered girls."

Alissa said Colin had "a delicious mouth" and recalled how they had massaged each other with creams.

"He looked completely white, soft and sandy-haired," she said. "He smeared my elbows with body lotion. Then I hung over him and massaged his back."

In the end Colin posed with Alissa as another naked lady, with just a towel around her head, snapped pictures of them.

"I liked him very much indeed and it was a very sexy interview."

Colin has since married his TV co-star, Liza Goddard.

When I asked him about the magazine interview, he said: "Absolutely no comment whatsoever."

Alissa's interview with star racing driver James Hunt was at his Spanish villa in Marbella.

"James was also very nice," she reported. "But I couldn't possibly compare him with Colin — they aren't at all the same."

James, formerly married to model girl Suzy Miller, who later married Richard Burton, admi[illegible]

surprise at Alissa's unorthodox interviewing methods.

He told a friend that he wondered why she insisted on being in all the poolside shots with him.

"I wasn't bothered that she wanted to be in the picture," said James.

"It was when she pulled off her blouse and I got nipples all over my elbows that I realised it wasn't going to be just another feature."

Never one to give up easily, James agreed to carry on with the assignment.

Eager

Next day a British motor magazine reported him as being "a mixture of quiet confidence and eager anticipation" about Alissa's sex rating of him.

"I was on good form," he said. "But I have to wait to read my official ratings."

Every month Alissa is given a generous expense account and air tickets to wherever she thinks her next quarry might be.

"I write about everything," she said. "And I never plan anything.

"I never plan to go to bed with the man I interview. I just wait and see what happens," she said. "But I enjoy my [illegible] very much."

JAMES HUNT: Suprised by Alissa's methods

NAKED truth: Alissa interviews Colin at the sauna. "I'm glad you undressed firs[t] luckily he doesn't do that. His house is beautiful, though not cosy. It is rented and it contains furniture belonging to other people: a deep sofa made of light material with orange and green flowers on it. There are some photographs of James in his racing car, which remind me of a boy's room.

'Do you think of yourself as a boy or a man?'

'A boy,' he says quickly. 'That is logical because all my life I have done nothing else than having fun. I have never outgrown it.'

'You have worked hard as well, haven't you?'

'Yes, very hard. I have been working as a professional driver for 11 years and have only started earning money the last three.'

'The last two years I have started to see myself as a woman.'

'How old are you?'

'Thirty-one.'

'I'm twenty-nine. Maybe in two years time I will feel like a man. I find it very strange turning thirty. Odd, to feel that you are still a boy ...'

He has undressed and gets into the bath that he has filled in the meantime. I have put the lid of the toilet down so I can sit on it.

'Do you mind looking the other way?' asks James, when he stands up in the bath to wash himself. 'Otherwise I will become very shy.'

'Yes,' I say, smiling because the wall opposite the bath consists entirely of mirrors. James is laughing too.

'Now I'm ready for everything,' says James, after he has put his clean cloths on, combed his hair and has put a necklace with a coin around his neck. We will be going out to dinner with two friends of his. James and I are sitting on the back seats of their car. During the drive he puts his hand on my knee. Softly he begins to tickle my thighs – he has the courage to do that!!

'All day, I have been looking at your legs,' he says. I have to laugh about his. 'You are stroking nicely,' I say.

'I would like to stroke you all over your body.'

'That sounds wonderful.'

While we are sitting at the bar in the restaurant, my legs are being tickled again.

'I am doing it in a way that nobody will notice.'

'I actually find it nice when people can see,' I say. That comment makes James laugh. 'But doing this in secret is nice too. Is it possible to stroke my legs when we are sitting at our table?'

James was on the front page again, and for a very unusual reason: the seductress had struck (courtesy Nieuwe Revue).

Enjoyment, enjoyment!

That is exactly what he does even while we are having a serious conversation, poker faced.

Later on, when we are lying on the bed, I hold James to his promise.

All of which leads to a provocative thought (as if all of this isn't provocative enough already). Ms Morrien did NOT award marks for style and technical merit, at least in this feature article. So, James, I know it's very late and I know you won't ever read this but ... you might have got those two 10s if she had awarded marks. Hope you did.

JUST JAMES

The memories in this final mosaic have been selected to complement those in the opening chapter. After Hunt retired from driving, Marlboro took him on as an adviser because the company had an extensive involvement in motorsport at all levels.

ALLAN McNISH

The Marlboro World Championship team was the young driver programme. The year I did it the team comprised Jean Alesi and Volker Wielder in Formula 3000, Eddie Irvine and JJ Lehto in Formula 3, Mika Häkkinen and me in Vauxhall Lotus. Then I progressed to Formula 3 with Mika and Formula 3000 with Erik Comas.

James came to the majority of our races and he was there as an adviser. If I had any problems I'd phone him up on occasions and ask him. That might be about circuits, about situations, if I had a problem with the team how to approach it, if I had a problem with the car, or if he had an opinion on what I needed to change in my lifestyle. It was whatever it may be. Then he gave his opinion and you know James, he always gave it in a rather forthright manner.

I don't think you can be in the Diplomatic Service, to be honest. He gave it straight from the heart, he gave it as he believed it and as he saw it. It was exactly like he gave his opinions on TV in the Grand Prix coverage in that he was commentating on you a little bit. The thing about him was that he had some real nuggets of information, absolute nuggets and, although some of it was irrelevant, if you sifted through you could pick up something which, in 30 years of racing, you wouldn't have heard from anyone else. He was very, very sharp.

I was in awe of James at the beginning because I was 17 years old. He was on television Grand Prix coverage, he was the last British World Champion at that point, instantly recognisable and instantly heard! The first time I met him he was with Hughes de Chaunac, Mike Earle and Graham Bogle[1], deciding on whether I got the chance to move forward in my career or not. So from that side he was a big man in so many ways and I *was* a little bit in awe of him. Then over a period of time I realised he was slightly eccentric but underneath it all he was actually a nice and genuine guy. Something I don't think people really understood was how level the playing field in his mind really was.

Technically he could watch me and tell me where I was going wrong, and he instinctively knew when you should do or say something.

I was watching some of the coverage of Monaco Grand Prix on one of the television channels a couple of weeks ago [the incident mentioned in the chapter Pure Fear?] and it was a good reminder of him and his basic theory of life: if there is an issue you hit it head on. You don't go around and about it, you don't talk around and about it, you just hit it head on. That's the way you get it solved quickly.

The thinking racing driver (Getty Images).

PERRY McCARTHY

Obviously there was a self-destruct element but a mischievous side as well, looking for fun. You'd be thinking, *right, here's a whole bundle of fun waiting to happen – or is he already in the middle of it?*

We were out in Sicily, coming back from Enna and a Formula 3000 race, and James was out there working on behalf of Marlboro. I wasn't racing, I was beating somebody's brains out to try and get a drive – as normal. There was a pack of drivers who were in the race. We all got on the plane and suddenly James arrived. First off, he had already obviously started on the happy juice.

A week before his first race in a Grand Prix car he took the Surtees TS15 to Mallory Park in the opening Formula 2 event of the season, but a suspension problem halted him (LAT Photographic).

Secondly, he was holding a helium parrot-shaped balloon which was up in the air as he got on the plane. Thirdly, he had in tow – by the arm – a young lady who was built fairly well but looked as if she had been round the circuit more than James had.

We're already having a look at this bird he'd got. He's spotted a load of people looking round as he and this lady have taken their seats. After about ten seconds, James was moved to stand up and address his comments to the rest of the cabin. It went as follows: 'look' – in his upper class, clipped accent – 'look, I know she may not be great to look at but she's got fabulous tits, don't you think?' We were wetting ourselves laughing. She was going, in an East End accent, 'aw, James, stop it, sit *dahn*, stop it, James.'

That was just James all over. It's a beautiful story because it's exactly him. James got away with it out of sheer charm and charisma.

At Birmingham, in Formula 3000, I had gone in pretty damn hard [but failed to qualify for the race]. I was furious about a million different things. Anyway, I was at the bar having a beer and James came straight up to me. He said 'Perry, Perry, you're one of the boys. Where are the women?'

MARCUS PYE

Motorsport journalist

At the McLaren *Autosport* young driver event at Silverstone he was McLaren's man. He pitched up and then cleared off at about ten o'clock in the morning before a wheel had turned. He came back half cut about half past five and said 'well, I don't know what's happened, so you boys had better choose!' I think he'd been to see some budgie breeder mate in Towcester. Unbelievable!

And he pitched up at Pau in '87 with some bird, and he was looking after the Marlboro drivers. He was so drunk he climbed on the bus to Pau airport with a ghetto blaster on his shoulder against his ear and that really irritated everybody because he wouldn't turn the bloody thing down. He was odious in the extreme, but other times he was great fun.

He was a hooligan. I mean, you probably haven't pissed on the curtain between first class and steerage on an aircraft, have you? Presumably he wasn't aware that he was doing it.

GEOFF RUMBLE

OK, he was World Champion but if he'd been a calmer character he'd have passed unnoticed in spite of his World Championship. Not many people talk about, say, Denny Hulme[2] these days, do they? He was a much quieter guy.

JOHN WATSON

He was a very complex man with a party animal side to him, which was completely contrasted by when he had his children with Sarah. The public didn't see that. And he had his bloody budgies!

I do think he had his moment on the road to Damascus in the late 1980s or the early '90s. It was almost like those people who go off to India to find themselves. His drinking and his basic lifestyle was seriously out of control and I think he was being given a red card by a few people close to him.

In 1990 suddenly *Eurosport* appeared on the horizon

Hunt addresses a meeting in London on sportsmanship, 1981 – and he's holding the railing on the stand, not driving it (Getty Images).

'Plums', the beautiful still life painting by artist Helen Dyson, which gave Hunt so much pleasure (courtesy Helen Dyson).

[with Grand Prix coverage, Watson giving expert analysis and comment]. While it was never a threat or a challenge to the BBC on a numbers basis, there was an alternative broadcast. I noticed a change in terms of his suddenly realising that, and maybe it contributed.

CHRIS MARSHALL

It's hard to analyse but I think he concentrated so much on what he was doing when he was racing. Once he'd stopped, his life took on a slightly different aspect, and then he got married for the second time, which obviously was different to the first. She was tremendous fun.

He did have a lined face at the end. I think the training contributes to that as well as everything else. They have to keep very fit and tend to get lined faces with the effort, especially with the neck exercises. He did keep fit. He was a runner – a lot of people jog but he could run.

I used to be a cyclist in my youth and when he first did *Superstars* he consulted me about the best way to do the cycling event. I discussed the height of the saddle and getting the handlebars correct so that he was comfortable on the bike. I taught him how to pull up when you've got your feet in the clip as well as push down on the other pedal when you're accelerating. I taught him to ride in a straight line rather than wobble about all over the place. He would take that advice and was determined to improve his performance in each sector. That was his competitive instinct coming out.

A Bohemian public schoolboy just drifting through? I suppose you've got to relax. Like a golfer or a tennis player, anybody who's up at that level the whole time had to have some downtime. Otherwise you'll blow up.

He certainly didn't do things to provoke a reaction. He was natural. He had his own group of friends away from racing, some from school and some from soon after, who he would retreat to, if you like, and with them he didn't come the high and mighty World Champion. If he did he'd get a rice pudding over his head. I'm absolutely sure that kept him level headed and sure footed, and equally with this coterie of friends he expected everybody to contribute. It wasn't as if he was the guru and everybody tagged along behind, as I've seen with lots of other people. If you were part of James's set you contributed and everybody did contribute.

He hated a lot of the posing. He hated all forms of posing and also the PR side. Of course in his Formula 1 contracts he had to do a certain amount. I remember once – at a dinner at the Grosvenor House – Bubbles, James and myself were in the lavatory signing autographs because I used to do all the entry forms for James, I used to do a perfectly good facsimile of his signature, and so could Bubbles. So we're signing autographs for this dinner, all three of us going at it. Anyone who's got one doesn't know if it's the genuine article. I'd like to say mine is just as valuable as his!

His theory was that if he was sitting down at dinner and he'd got a jacket on then nobody would know that he had jeans and tennis shoes underneath. It was two fingers to officialdom really, and to inane activity which so many people go through, and the rigmarole, what you're expected to do for PR, advertising of the sponsors – which was terribly boring and a real waste of time as far as James was concerned. But of course he did it, and he did it as quickly and easily as he could.

He gave a lecture once and he stood behind the lectern wearing a jacket and a bow tie, but of course he'd got the jeans and the tennis shoes below that. Nobody could see them. I suppose that gave him a bit of satisfaction.

PERRY McCARTHY

I never thought too much about James's background. I used to love his accent. To me he encapsulated somebody who was very confident, very self-assured but had a charm about him and also was, to a large degree, a bloke's bloke. Most of my mates in motor racing are exactly the same. As far as careers are concerned, everybody is super determined and highly focused and result driven, and James certainly fitted into that. You just don't make it if you're not.

Life has changed since then. Even I've worked with the computers and so on, which James and that lot didn't do. To be fast you have to understand the race car and work with the engineers and he was certainly bright enough to do all that. It's just that the resources available at that time were more human communication. *Let's try this, let's try that, is it working? It shows up on the stopwatch after a lap.* Maybe they were sophisticated enough to do a couple of split times but pretty much that was it.

I think James being physically sick before some of the races was nerves, nerves of anticipation, of knowing what he was going to do. There was an interesting moment in a DVD of Le Mans I was watching the other night. Just before the race there's a part where we're skipping to different drivers getting ready in their little caravans. An Italian, good looking lad, is suddenly in front of the mirror and he's just adjusting himself but then he looked into the mirror.

There are so many tiny moments at Le Mans and as a race driver I picked them up.

The Italian looked in the mirror and in spirit I was there with him because I know what that is: you are looking at this guy who is yourself and you are disassociating yourself from him. There's the face you know so well and there's a voice saying *what are you going to do today? How far are you going to go?* And *are we going to see each other again?* That was that moment on the DVD, because I know what that moment is like. It's just a look in the mirror but also a moment of connection with yourself. I think that James saw that in his time.

Outside the cockpit I have questioned myself many times about what I have done in it just before – if I regarded it as pretty dumb or too chancy. I have questioned myself when I am going to get into the cockpit: *how am I going to do all that nonsense again?* But the thing is, no matter how nervous and agitated you may be – and my supposition applies to James as well – when you put the crash helmet on that's it, *because now you have to get on with the deal.* He might have been shaking or throwing up, but the moment he was in the car he was then in *his* environment. One day if you're still shaking and throwing up when you *are* in the car, it's time to leave.

James wasn't relaxed about what he was going to do, he wasn't like on a fairground ride – oh, it's all going to be a laugh. He had that level of expectation in him, as top drivers do, because they say: *I want this and I need this and I am going to very big heights to achieve this.* That's where the apprehension comes from because you know, from being a terribly competitive person, that is exactly where you are going to be putting yourself.

It's very difficult to generalise with race drivers but the thing I connect with James about is that people have accused me of race-day moodiness. I don't want to talk with people much, don't want to use a lot of energy doing that, my mind is somewhere else. Some other people, maybe they are totally OK.

There's an analogy here. Certain comedians – like Tommy Cooper – when they come on you start laughing

Continued on page 140

THE STARS IN HUNT'S ORBIT

James Hunt knew the stars and the stars knew James Hunt because he was one of them.

ROGER MOODY

We were doing a preview to the first Caesars Palace Grand Prix [at Las Vegas in 1981]. James came out on the Saturday and as part of the preview I'd arranged for him to do an interview with Sammy Davis Jnr that night – he was headlining at Caesars Palace. Then we were going to go round the track with Carlos Reutemann on the Sunday in a car. Anyway I met James on the Saturday morning.

Moody: 'James, good to see you, mate. This is what I want you to do today and I'll see you tonight for the Sammy Davis Jnr interview.'

Hunt: 'No.'

Moody: 'This is what we've got organised.'

With a little help from my friends. Beatles star George Harrison was a good chum and a genuine motor racing supporter (LAT Photographic).

Hunt: 'No, I'm not doing that. You see this young lady behind me? I've met her in Los Angeles on the way up here. We are going to my room and I'll see you tomorrow morning.'

And that's what happened. And guess who got to interview Sammy Davis Jnr? Me. So there was a plus to that ...

For James it was *Sammy Davis Jnr, so what?* That was his ultimate charm but it was also, I have to say, extremely unprofessional of him by virtue of the fact that he was being paid by the BBC to be out there, not cavorting around with someone he'd picked up in Los Angeles. But without that sort of story about James, where would the folklore be?

PETER WARR

He and Sean Connery used to play golf when James had *Oscar's*, the nightclub down in Marbella. They used to go out and pretend to the tourists they couldn't play – and finish up playing for 200 or 300 quid.

Incidentally, the golf club wouldn't allow Oscar on the golf course so James bought him a membership. The dog duly became a member and naturally could go on the course. That was James.

NOEL EDMONDS

I feel very honoured that I met him and I was desperately sad about his early demise. I personally found him charismatic, charming and fun – and looking back on it, even though he very nearly killed us it's one on my CV: I've flown with the Red Arrows, I've done this, I've done that and I've been on a rally with James Hunt!

JOHN WEBB

In 1976, to publicise the Grand Prix at Brands Hatch, we hired the Albert Hall and we put on a night of the stars, which included most of the Grand Prix drivers. Shirley Bassey was top of the bill and I recall James played the trumpet that night.

A former Daily Express colleague of mine, John Lloyd, was close to Ms Bassey so I asked him to investigate. This is what he sent me:

Now listen, sunshine … comedian Eric Morecambe made people laugh – including Hunt (LAT Photographic).

'Sexy James Hunt sent hearts racing in Shirley Bassey's dressing room when they appeared at a prestigious fund-raiser for the British Grand Prix at London's Royal Albert Hall. Shirley's camp couturier Doug Darnell proudly recalls his encounter with Hunt the Hunk in those dark, narrow corridors underneath the big Albert Hall stage.

'He was wearing skin-tight jeans and an open shirt, revealing his six-pack midriff! As I was carrying Shirley's dress, I had to say "excuse me, please" as he brushed against me and we nearly got stuck.

'Mr Hunt flashed his famous wide smile and that sent me weak at the knees. I couldn't get back to the dressing room quick enough to boast to Shirley that I'd just been in a crush with the most beautiful blond MAN in the world! No wonder the gay papers voted James Hunt No.1 dream boy for years.

'Shirley and I have no secrets. She often introduced me to close friends like Barbara Windsor and Roger Moore and wife Dorothy Squires as "this is lovely Doug. He's camper than a row of tents – as if you didn't know!"

'But after my unexpected meeting with famed womaniser Mr Hunt, Shirley could see I was near collapse. I had heard insiders whisper "anything on legs and Hunt is chasing it, without waiting for the hounds!"

'He certainly had huge appeal for both sexes. When Shirley heard of my all-too-brief encounter, she fixed me with her hometown Tiger Bay, Cardiff stare and shrieked "I'll let you into a little secret, Doug. I saw him first, so eyes and hands off. He's MINE."

'Before going on stage Shirley kept my pro-Hunt temperature high by saying "and another thing, Doug … James also blows a hot trumpet!"'

JOHN WEBB

James was at Brands doing a TV commercial with Arthur Daley and they both got into such a fit of laughter that they couldn't complete the commercial – so there was a very human side to James.

Doug Darnell and Shirley Bassey, April 1960. Both had weak knees when they passed Hunt the Hunk (Hulton Archive).

before they ever get to the middle of the stage. If you liked James, the moment you saw him you'd be smiling thinking *what's he up to?* He had a mischievous side to him, you see.

At the end maybe he was bored. You've got someone who was full of tension, hyperactive and a high achiever in an environment where things were going on with him at the centre at a million miles an hour. You take that person out of that environment and if you don't put them into business or any other demanding activity what happens? You stay at a million miles an hour and you start attacking the only thing that you've got left, which is you. And I know a bit about this – that's why I'm in business and doing deals and keeping moving and everything else. Post motor racing, my brain is still one million miles an hour on anything I want to achieve.

I think that was the problem with James. And what's left? Boredom and then depression, because financially it all started going wrong. Then you attack yourself even harder. I am not trying to be a psychoanalyst, I'm not bright enough, but that's how I see it.

JEAN MORGAN

Wife of racing driver Dave

I only know what I saw on a particular day at Brands Hatch. The boys [Freddie and Tom] would come in and James could be talking to anybody and they'd just climb all over him. He seemed to have unlimited patience. He was obviously quite devoted to them and it was sincere, oh yes. Having seen his wild side I was pleasantly surprised – and pleased for the boys that, after he died, they would have nice memories. I think that's very important. In the early days he had totally no regard for anything conventional – or *anything*. Look at the time when he was invited to dinner at the RAC Club and he turned up in jeans and a tee-shirt – total disregard for anybody. What was that? I have no idea, no idea.

SARAH LOMAX

When we separated he'd always come round on the boys' birthday and play Happy Birthday on his trumpet on Wimbledon Common so they could hear it. Wonderful. He was an incredible father and the shame is that that was taken away, because people would have seen the real James in the years to come, as I saw him. He was the doting dad, focussed, unbelievably patient, more patience than I've got. Doing something with the boys he was down to their eye level, he never talked down to them, he'd always kneel. Sometimes you're taught to do that but he knew that instinctively.

BOB CONSTANDUROS

Motorsport journalist

I wasn't really a contemporary in the way that Ian Phillips and Chris Witty were. I only really knew James afterwards when he was a driver-coach for Marlboro. I saw him all the way through from his particularly wild days when he was with some pretty awful women – say in Pau and places like that – to when he was all cleaned up and with his final lady.

I particularly remember the European Grand Prix at Donington on that Easter Sunday in 1993 – a filthy day. We had to do a presentation at some hotel at the East Midlands airport and we were *yomping* across the fields because they had failed to come and pick us up. James was in full flow about the grid and this and that, all sorts of things and people. He was in really good form and he looked very fit.

He was pretty forthright – well, very opinionated. He was going to be right. It wasn't really a discussion with him, it was *this is the way it is*. And it didn't matter what the subject was, whether it was about racing or anything else. On this particular day – I would not call him a friend, because he wasn't necessarily a friendly type – he was closer. In fact he was friendly with a small number of people and that was it.

We did chat sometimes, not very much and it was a one-way chat.

I don't think he played on the public schoolboy, that's just the way he was, wouldn't have made any difference where he'd gone to school, to be honest.

PATRICK TAMBAY

I don't know what happened at the end of his life, but what I do know – from having him as a team-mate at McLaren – is that he was a nice human being, no, a lovely human being.

LORD HESKETH

I think towards the end he was much more at peace with himself. He was a complicated guy. For all these guys, all sportsmen, it's changed quite a lot in the sense that there is life afterwards. There's a senior tour, there's $10m in the bank and there's also an awful lot of money in Grand Prix racing. You go up to the paddock at Silverstone and there is a large number of modestly unemployable people who are all rather well paid to just sort of float around and hand out presents. This applies to all sports, not just motor racing. A lot of guys, suddenly they're 35, 38 and it's *not* Monday morning, off testing, it's 'I haven't had a chance to learn any profession or even meet people beyond motorsport and the best I'm going to be offered is someone who's quite keen on racing saying would I like the chance to be an insurance broker?' It was a different world. The opportunities were very limited then, compared to today.

He was the kind of guy you'd be perfectly happy going tiger shooting with because he had a combination of competence and bravery.

TAORMINA RIECK

It was almost as if his life went in a full circle and he came back to being the person that I met when I was 13-ish. He went through all the traumas, all the ups and the downs but certainly the last time I saw him I thought 'gosh, it's the old James back again.' I think he was at peace with himself. He had found happiness with Helen.

Dear old James ... he was something different, something special and I was really happy at the end to see him sitting there not smoking, not drinking, and doting on his sons. I remember sometimes going and babysitting when he and Sarah had had the boys. I'd go round and he would always read them a story and say their prayers with them.

I suppose he'd had a good grounding and he carried that on when they were his. He knew what to do and it

In lifestyle, he suited Monaco and Monaco suited him although he never won there. The flag marshal seems to know that and isn't impressed. This is 1976 (LAT Photographic).

wasn't strange to him. He was a loving brother too. There was also the fact that they were boys. I think he'd probably have been very good with girls but I dread to think what would have happened if he'd had a girl and she'd got to the teenager stage and boyfriends had appeared! *Don't you lay a hand on my daughter ...*

The real James was a very genuine person. I have always said that his life was in three stages really: the growing up and the getting into motor racing until he got there, and then when he got there until he finished motor racing, and then afterwards the commentating. The first and last stages were far more the same person, and the person in the middle wasn't really him. He was almost a creation of other people. When he made it, it was great fun at first. There was the cash and women and wow! But that wasn't really him.

It was interesting that he kept his old friends, the old group from home, from Sutton and Cheam. We still see each other and in fact a load of us met up the other day and James and Malcolm Wood have both died with heart problems. The rest of us met and we feel that we are an incredibly lucky bunch because we have remained friends.

I remember the fun times we all had. Actually this dinner we went to the other day with this Cheam lot. Somebody raked out an old photo: someone's 21st. There they all were, James dressed in his dinner jacket looking smart. Oh yes, when he was young he conformed, and when he put it on he looked good.

PROFESSOR SID WATKINS

Formula 1 medical supremo

My strongest memory? Tremendous fun, very intelligent, fascinating sense of humour, very irreverent. Quite sort of mischievous. For example after a race I've seen him dragging two black bin bags around, one full of cans of beer and the other full of empty cans of beer – as he had a few after the race. I remember him getting on a carousel at an airport in the luggage and going round and round, coming out through those rubber slats. One night we were flying back – I think it must have been some sort of charter – and he got hold of the PA. He started to perform in pseudo-German, instructing various people to do certain tasks and that was very, very funny.

So he was a great, mischievous chap but awfully polite and respectful as far as I was concerned. He was very good at the circuits in terms of behaving himself in the paddock, apart from the way he used to dress.

He was a very sensible guy in many ways although he was naughty with the weed, wasn't he? It might have been an escape mechanism from the tension.

Helen Dyson came to Coldstream a couple of times with him. When he retired from driving I saw him because he was commentating. Then we got this house in Scotland with some fishing in 1987. It was after that that he started to come up. I invited him and he came up on his own. Then he asked if he could bring his little boys and they used to come. We had a very large twin-bedded room and I think one of them was small enough to go on a mattress on the floor. James looked after them brilliantly. He'd get up early with them and cook their breakfasts. He'd make toast soldiers to dip into the yolks of the eggs. He was an absolutely marvellous father. This was not the public persona at all.

I had one rod on the Tweed so he would take that and go fishing with the gillie and I'd take the two little boys with two little trout rods and we'd fool around in the pools. He could fish but I don't think he ever caught anything. He loved it. I felt perfectly relaxed with him, oh, absolutely. Good pals. He never tried to be anything but himself. He'd go off to the local pub and have a few pints with the pal who was a gillie. If my youngsters were up they'd all go off together. He was completely unaffected – there was no pretension about him whatsoever.

HELEN DYSON

Fiancée

It's like someone suddenly becomes public property just because they happen to have been famous, but that had nothing to do with my life with James. We lived a very quiet, normal, bog-standard life and a very happy one. We were madly in love but lived a normal existence. It wasn't all a – I don't know what people think – jet set, racy kind of life. I didn't know any of that previous life so it's all very abstract to me. You might as well be talking about another person.

We didn't really go out very much, our house was our castle. We took the dogs out quite a lot on the common and went cycling but really normal stuff – going to the supermarket. It wasn't going to flashy restaurants. We didn't do anything like that. He didn't want to and I didn't want to. We just pottered around and had a lovely time in our house together. He worked from home doing his writing and I was in the studio and we were very at one with the world.

It was terribly secluded, it wasn't overlooked and we were private.

There'd be about 200 budgies – well, the most would be 200. They were very important to him. He got sick of it by the end and actually sold them. He'd had enough. He took it seriously and he was competitive.

I'd like to say how generous he was towards me. When I sold my first painting he was much happier about it than I was, he was just ecstatic. He said 'I've had my career, now it's your turn.' He was so, so, into my art. That was very special. That was all new to him and he tried so hard, he was so giving. He was putting me first. People wouldn't have known that. All he wanted was for me to do my painting.

This is just so James. There's a beautiful, big book on Raoul Dufy,[3] he's as famous as Matisse, he's a very famous

The inscription James wrote.

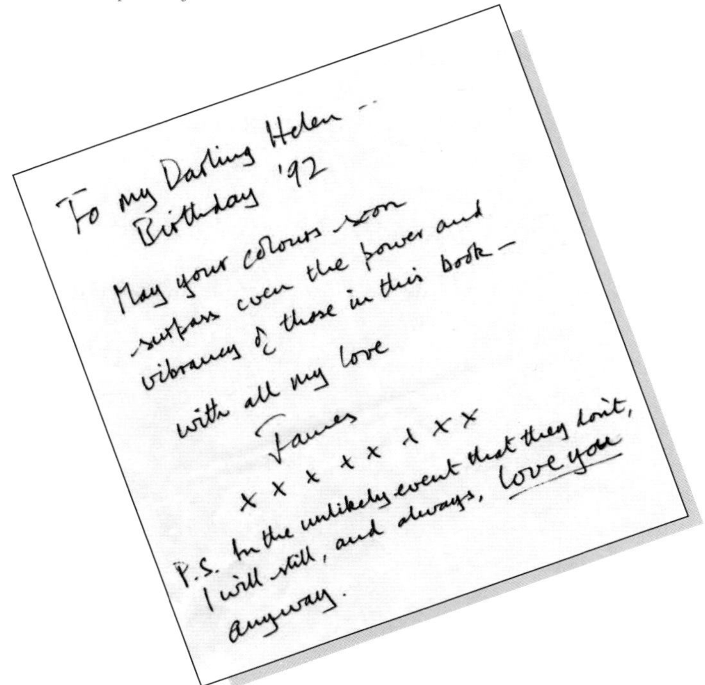

To my Darling Helen –
Birthday '92
May your colours soon
surpass even the power and
vibrancy of those in this book –
with all my love
James
x x x x x x x x
P.S. In the unlikely event that they don't,
I will still, and always, love you
anyway.

Rare visit to a nightclub in 1992 for domestic couple James Hunt and Helen Dyson (Richard Young/Rex Features).

artist and he did very, very colourful work. James bought it and signed it *My darling Helen, birthday, 1992. May your colours soon surpass even the power and vibrancy of these in this book. With all my love, James.*

PS In the unlikely event that they don't, I will still and always love you anyway.

Another book he got when he was in Barcelona for one of the races, an art book, on Gaudi.[4] *To my darling Helen, when we get to Barcelona together we can go and see in the flesh the works that we like here. Lots of love and happiness for you forever, James.*

PS I had so much fun buying the book. It was the climax of a really nice day and came as a surprise when I'd just about given up trying to find something. It really excited me.

We were madly in love. It was absolutely magical.

HOME SWEET HOME

NIGEL ROEBUCK

I went to his house lots and lots of times in Wimbledon, a beautiful house but just how you'd expect it to be with James living in it. Untidy. Oscar was always about and the budgies were there. He once gave me the conducted tour. I got there and he said 'you've arrived just at feeding time.' I don't know how many budgies he had and he'd have a little conversation with each of them. *You're looking a bit peaky today.* He adored these birds and he wouldn't be separated from Oscar.

It struck me that, for all his slightly patrician background and Wellington and everything else, he was a bohemian. When he was racing, I disliked almost everything about him – largely because of the entourage and how contrived that was, and frankly I thought a lot of the Hesketh stuff was contrived too. I remember once, in the Press Room, Alan Henry had just been through this performance with the entourage and he was saying something about public school twits and everything else. It was probably to some degree said for my benefit because I'd gone to public school too, and I can remember saying to him 'it's people like that who give public schools a bad name. I understand why people respond as they do if they think that's a typical public schoolboy.'

Once James stopped racing, he really was a true bohemian. I also think he was, in his way, a true eccentric. I have always said that of all the eccentrics I have ever met there was Jenks [Denis Jenkinson] and nobody near him, but I do think James was a true eccentric as well. It wasn't contrived.

For example, in this house in Wimbledon was a parrot whose name I can't remember and it had the bluest vocabulary I have ever heard. It was like a Liverpool docker. I don't think he'd taught the parrot, it had just picked it all up from the conversations it heard. Of course it wasn't in a cage, it just flew around – a bohemian parrot as well …

In the end, it was all bricks and mortar at Wimbledon (News (UK) Limited/Rex Features).

He had this black ... well, not exactly manservant, but this guy who worked for him who had been a minicab driver, and had taken James so often that they got to know each other. Winston, he was called. Winston had become pretty well a permanent feature. James would ring the minicab company and ask for Winston and Winston would be sent and eventually Winston finished up working for James.

I was there one Saturday afternoon and James was pretty well out of booze. He said, 'Ah, Winston, your master's going to give you a *century*. With this he requires three bottles of vodka, two bottles of ...' and he ran through the list. Then Winston departed in the A35 van to get it.

MICK MAPSTON

Budgerigar breeder

Winston was like a nanny, wasn't he? He was always dressed in leather. The parrots didn't like him much. James had two parrots, one called Saddam and one called Hussein. No surprise at that, really, is there? Winston used to walk around with a golf club because they sensed that he was a bit wary of them and at any opportunity they'd try and have a little go at him. James used to say 'Winston walks around with a golf club most of the day in case he gets attacked.' I think they were spiteful in general so they'd probably have had a go at most people. If I remember rightly, one was being groomed for stardom because it had done auditions for a stage play, might have been *Treasure Island*. They wanted a parrot for Long John Silver! And James wanted to get his bird onto the stage. It was a stand-in, I don't think it actually got the part ...

Winston made West Indian cocktails, had a bit of rum in them and this sort of thing, and they were quite potent. I seem to remember that.

WINSTON TOMLINSON

General factotum

No, no, no, no, no! He only had one parrot and it was called Humbert.

SALLY HUNT

It's the family parrot, my parents' parrot, and it's about 39 years old. It goes round the family and we have it from time to time. James particularly enjoyed the parrot.

WINSTON TOMLINSON

As far as I know, he was looking after another two for somebody – they were not exactly parrots, they look like parrots but they don't have the same colour. Those two: one *was* called Saddam and one called Hussein.

Did I go round with a golf club? Not really! Not really. No, no, no, no! I don't know nothin' about that!

I didn't find anything eccentric about him, really, for me personally I didn't see anything eccentric. I saw him as just being a normal person. I didn't see him doing anything out of the ordinary.

I used to work for a taxi company and I lost my licence around 1984, 1985. I had ferried him about a bit, oh yes. We did a lot of ferrying about. When I lost it he said 'come and do a bit of domestic work around the house, the garden and things like that until you get your licence back.' So it was only a temporary thing but it became permanent! He tried to look after me. So I did the garden and looked after the kids, do a little bit of cookin' for him sometimes.

Fried chicken, Jamaica style?

I don't know about that! It was with red wine, could be known as English, could be known as American – but it all went down.

I found him more on the spiritual side. Some others may have found him different but personally I found that. There *was* a spiritual side to him. He had a sense of humour and the same things made us both laugh. If he felt somebody had upset him he would say it straight out. There's nothing wrong about that. That's why I liked him so much because he didn't bottle it up, he'd talk about it and that would be it. Did he ever tell me off? He gave me **** plenty of times! I didn't take it too seriously because I knew that's how he is and he'd forget about it two minutes later.

ALAN JENKINS

We'd go up to Wimbledon and his house was amazing. It was a true open house – people, dogs, whatever, all trooped in and out. I remember going with our dog and of course we lived in the countryside, we never had dog leads or anything like that. The dog walked in, cocked its

Continued overleaf

Continued from previous page

leg and peed on James's telly. Normally you'd die of embarrassment, wouldn't you? He didn't bat an eyelid. *Dogs do that all the time.*

I was in the Marlboro family, if you like, from my original McLaren days so I saw a lot of him. He socialised there and he was a very welcome guest.

JOHN BLUNSDEN

I'd been to his place in Wimbledon and at a time when, yes, he had looked a bit dissipated. I only went there once, actually. He had a black manservant – Winston – and he had this rather dilapidated looking Merc, up on blocks in the front garden, and his budgies of course. Fairly chaotic sort of place really. He was slightly bohemian in that sense.

TAORMINA RIECK

One of the last times I saw him was at Wimbledon. I phoned him up and said 'can I park my car in your drive?' He said 'well, if it's raining I'll have to charge you.' I said 'bloody hell, you old stingy creature!' If it had been raining, the car parks would have been full and he could have let out the space to any old passer by, so he didn't want to lose the money. I turned up with my eldest daughter and there he was, shoeless as always. It was about the time he was supposed to do a drive with Williams but he couldn't fit in the car. It was very sad to see someone who couldn't afford the Merc – there it was up on the bricks. It was just like he was in the early days. If we went out anywhere, it was a question of *everyone hands in pockets* because James couldn't afford it: every penny went on another spare part or whatever. Did he charge me? No he didn't! It wasn't raining. I will never know if he would have charged me!

He was happy, he had his parrot and his budgerigars and the dog. We went in and it was actually very much like the home he grew up in. Comfortable – chaotic but comfortable. Not smart in the slightest, but that wasn't James. Helen was there, sound asleep upstairs so we didn't see her on that occasion. It was back to the beginning again, no money but happy.

BRIAN HENTON

I think he was great, absolutely great. He was a total one-off. He never seemed to train or anything, like everybody else, yet he could still play squash to almost international level, then he could run down the road for five or six miles even though he smoked like a chimney. He had these rounded shoulders which were so powerful it was untrue.

We were always mates, actually. I was known as Superhen, cock of the north. Dunno what that meant! Actually they christened me that when I went to a company called GRD which was built up by ex-Lotus people. It was actually called Griston Racing Developments and we all called it Griston Racing Disasters, because that's what it was.

The last time I saw James we'd both retired. He was commentating. On the Gloucester Road there's this steak house with a big Red Indian outside. I'm walking across the road and who should be walking the other way but Hunt! This is about one o'clock in the morning, with a fantastic blonde on his arm [Helen].

Hunt: '******* hell, Superhen, what are you doing here?'

Henton: 'I'm bloody taking over London. I'm buying up property left, right and centre!'

Hunt: 'Bloody great to see you.'

So, one o'clock in the morning and we reminisced. We'd both had a few vinos. He'd got his arm round the blonde. I will always remember him waving and saying 'see you soon.' Shortly after that he was dead.

At the end of the day, to become World Champion you've got to be good. You can't fluke that. I know what the game's like and James had the talent and, believe it or not, he had the dedication because if he hadn't he wouldn't have got there. He could do it when he wanted to – but he wanted to do it on his own terms, and he was probably one of the last who could afford to do it like that. The corporate thing would crush him totally now. And remember he had a wonderful benefactor in Alexander who gave him the push.

CHRIS MARSHALL

His mother said after he'd died that he crammed more into 45 years than most people do in an entire lifetime.

NICK BRITTAN

In his will he had set aside a sum of money and a set of very detailed instructions that upon his death, on the evening after his memorial service – which was a very splendid thing, and wasn't Alexander Hesketh absolutely wonderful? – there were to be two parties: one for the blue blazers at the RAC club, for which a small amount of money had been allocated, and one at the White Elephant [a restaurant] on the Embankment for which a much larger sum had been allocated, plus a list of his mates who were to be invited in order to become pissed. And that's what it was all about. His brother Pete ran the whole thing and everybody on the list got a letter saying *it is James's wish that you get pissed.*

CHRIS WITTY

James was loud but not outrageous. I always remember that when he died Peter said he had set some money aside to have a drink for his mates. I remember going to that and saying to a group *we must be the last to leave because that's the only way James would want it to be.* So people like Constanduros and Phillips and I sort of staggered into daylight and decided where we were going to go and have breakfast.

J. R. RICHARDSON

Who was James? Very, very late one night we were both in an appalling state and both having an extremely good time. This was The Meaning of Life conversation plus a lot of booze. He was one of the very, very, very few people that I could speak to and I *didn't* sense that I was getting to the real person. He always had a little barrier at the end. He could never, ever let go of all of himself. Maybe that was just me because I'm very upfront.

I said it to him about this barrier and he replied 'I am described as cold.' I'm not sure that actually he had the ability to open up. Some people don't, but very few. I would doubt whether anybody ever got that close,

The way so many fans remember the man – driving hard. Here, in a Marlboro McLaren, Hunt is winning the 1976 Race of Champions at Brands Hatch (Getty Images).

LAST PIT STOP

J. R. RICHARDSON

The weekend before he died we all had dinner together down at another mate of ours. It was at Purley, with Chris Jones and other people he'd known since he was 14 or 15. It was the last time I saw him. He looked better than he had for, I would say, at least three years. He was training and also his divorce was finished, which was a bloody, bloody awful, difficult time. He was devoted to the kids. I think he was one of the best fathers I've known. Everything focused around the kids.

Damaged himself so much? No, that's wrong. He died because of a congenital heart defect. Had it been spotted, had he gone for one of these ECGs, the weakness would have been spotted and he wouldn't have died. That's fact. We've all put a hell of a lot of mileage down but he was just unlucky. He was looking great, he was off everything.

SARAH LOMAX

I went up the day before he died and had tea with him. I said 'where does this come from?' and he said 'I just want to see you. Bring the boys up for tea.'

There was no suggestion he was ill, none whatsoever. He was in fine form.

In the early days, the BBC did not usually send their Grand Prix team to the distant races because these were not covered live. Instead, the team gathered at the BBC in London, Walker and Hunt commentated and then the highlights were spliced together for a later showing.

ROGER MOODY

When we weren't on site, James would cycle in from Wimbledon to Television Centre to do work and again you'd say 'where the hell is James?' He'd come ambling

A death in headlines.

DAILY Mirror

James Hunt..golden boy who lost it all

FAREWELL TO A HERO: A last picture shows ex-world champion James Hunt

END OF THE ROA

Sunday EXPRESS

JUNE 20, 1993 BRITAIN'S FASTEST GROWING QUALITY TABLOID 60p

COMFORTING ONE ANOTHER: Sarah with Tom, left, and Freddie. 'I'd like to be able to take all their pain . . . but they are going to have to deal with it,' she said

I promise James will be so proud of his little men

by John McEntee

The Daily Telegraph

partner of arm and avado

s, James Hunt's famous partnership ('The Good Lord', as Hunt called him) Formula One successes. It took him World Championship, which he won eth, now Government Chief Whip in ite to his friend, a British sporting rman, who died last Tuesday

friend, as well as a colleague in an enterprise which, although condemned at its inception by self-proclaimed cognoscenti as amateurish, became everything I might have wished of a Formula One équipe. Efficient but never hardfaced, competitive but never devious, stylish but never arrogant — James more than anyone in the team reflected this Corinthian ethos.

Lord Hesketh and James Hunt: a celebrated combination of owner and driver in, last minute. I remember in the days of film [pre digital] in the old Kensington House, which was the office building for the sports department, he used to come in with Oscar, the bloody dog, while we were putting motor racing films together in the cutting rooms, and the dog would crap all down the corridors. James didn't care but it was pretty horrendous for the rest of us. I don't know how he did get away with it.

The BBC, true to its public service remit, invited motor racing journalists to come and watch the coverage from these distant races, and many of the reports you read in the daily papers were put together like that. Two journalists, John Blunsden and Alan Brinton, accepted the invitation for the Canadian Grand Prix on Sunday, 13 June 1993.

JOHN BLUNSDEN

James and Murray were doing their usual double act, and doing it by remote control as they did on several occasions. Before the race James was on the phone to Gerry Donaldson, who was over in Montreal, and Gerry was feeding him all the background information about what had happened in the paddock and so on right up to the start of the race, so he was well-briefed. Then of course came the commentary.

I was doing *The Times* and Alan was doing the *Sun* or the *Telegraph*. The BBC used to give journalists the facility of watching the race because in those days it was difficult to find out what was going on and also we had tight deadlines. After James had finished talking to Gerry and I'd shouted 'give Gerry my best', James came out and said 'God, I'm busting for a Mars bar. Must go and find a Mars bar.' He rushed off and eventually found his Mars bar or two and came back. He went into the studio.

Here is an excerpt of what Blunsden and Brinton heard. You can hear the voices for yourself, repetitions, non-sequiturs, pauses and all.

Walker: 'He [Schumacher] is out on new, heated tyres almost up to race temperature, he knows the course and he knows with a clear track in front of him that he can get the pedal really hard down and try and catch Ayrton Senna ... as you watch Andretti and there was Ayrton Senna behind him. And into the pits comes Damon Hill from second position, so Ayrton Senna is up into second position in the McLaren. Let's see how long that pit stop is for Damon Hill. It's quite a long one because the right front is still not properly on. This is much too long a pit stop. Damon Hill has got some sort of a problem. This is very bad news. Seventeen seconds for Damon Hill. It should have been about seven seconds.'

Hunt: 'Yes, and it's hard to see what went wrong there but wrong it certainly went. At least ten seconds awry and there's been a bit of that this year with the very best teams having problems with wheels sticking on and things like that ... as Berger goes in for his tyre change. Now does this mean that Senna is going to stay out and try and run the race on one set of tyres – because it would be most uncharacteristic of him if he is planning to stop for tyres on a scheduled stop. He's still got a lot of laps to do in which he can change his mind, but if he was planning a definite scheduled stop, to let Schumacher and Hill get the jump on him, his immediate rivals, I would have thought was out of character. So I now have to think he now has to try and do the whole race [Senna angles McLaren into pitlane] but no, I'm getting everything wrong today, Murray. I am. And he's in. Good stop, this is an exceptional stop by McLaren. Senna is away and that should have him in second place.'

John Blunsden remembers Hunt being on good form.

I saw James just after the race and we exchanged a few words. He was bright, breezy and so on, his usual self. He said life was good. There was no question of him looking terribly drawn or haggard that night. He was fresh faced and full of the joys, as it were. He was going to get on his bike and cycle home.

He was a mixture. The trouble was – and whether he realised it, or realised the extent of it, I don't know – he was affected by the funny stuff. He had obviously been taking it for a long time and even though he'd shaken it off – because he'd probably had a few warnings – and superficially looked as if he was a fit man once again, I think unfortunately the damage had already been done internally. Nothing he could have done at that stage would have brought it back. It was a great, great shame.

James Hunt died of a heart attack two days later.

including his wives. In fact, his mates would have got closer than them.

I think there was something always held back, even to himself.

HUGH MACLENNAN

James could be very irritating but I miss him. I always thought that when the pop star thing had died down and he became more normal (!) I would contact him and perhaps we could re-establish our friendship. Of course, I regret not making an effort to contact him and to spend time with him. Yes, I miss him ... he was 'something else', as they say.

And the present, as well as the past.

SARAH LOMAX

James's second son, Freddie, has chosen polo as his career. He's gone on his second trip to Argentina [2005] for the work experience. It's where you go. He's gone for five months.

It's a most expensive sport. You need a minimum of eight horses and he needs sponsorship or he needs to have a lucky break – a patron – not dissimilar, I suppose, to James when Hesketh picked him up. And the polo? That's the danger and the competitive element coming out – the competitive element, absolutely.

Notes

1. Hughes de Chaunac, French racing team owner; Mike Earle, long-time motorsport activist in a variety of roles; Graham Bogle of Marlboro.
2. New Zealander and 1967 World Champion.
3. French painter Raoul Dufy helped 'to create a modern visual sensibility and perception, a way of seeing things after the First World War, which was different from the way they were ever seen before.' www.artcult.com/dufy.htm
4. Antoni Gaudí i Cornet (1852–1926) was at the forefront of the Art Nouveau movement in Spain. His work in Barcelona led to the creation of some of the city's most notable landmarks. Gaudí was a pioneer in his field using colour, texture, and movement in ways never before imagined. http://come.to/gaudi

THE OLD ENGLISH GENTLEMAN

Saffron Walden. The name is so evocative it even smells English, this market town nestling in the gentle, rolling countryside not far from Cambridge. By good fortune Taormina Rieck (nicknamed Ping), lives there and so does Tony Dron. I'm not far away and in late autumn 2005 we meet for lunch. Dron, most engaging of men, says he knows just the place, a pub in the town centre which does good food. The ground rules of our conversation: anyone can say anything and let's see where it goes.

DRON: I think there are loads of characters in modern day racing.

PING: You see them, Tony, because you're in there on the ground whereas Joe Public isn't allowed to see them.

CH: People now are not allowed to be characters because there is so much money involved in corporate imagery. In that sense we don't know if there are characters, whereas James would not have allowed that to happen.

DRON: That's perfectly true.

PING: But luckily I guess Marlboro had John Hogan there and he said 'OK, fine. If this is what we get, this is what we get.' And I think Hogan had the foresight to see the world didn't just want a plastic being, they wanted a character.

CH: But if they'd said 'James, you have to do this, James, you have to do that' they'd have been asking 'where's James gone?' – out the door, not coming back.

DRON: Things could have come to a halt for James quite easily at the end of the Hesketh era. It was most fortunate that that seat at McLaren came up at just the right time. Emerson went off to drive the Copersucar and McLaren needed a top man, a number one driver, very quickly. That was what gave James his opportunity.

CH: He didn't actually know how good he was at that stage because he'd never had a team-mate to compare himself with.

DRON: Well, yeah, but he'd been racing for a long time. He knew, really, in his heart.

CH: The first race in a McLaren he put it on pole and he suddenly realised he really could do this.

PING: Oh, I think he knew in his heart of hearts right from the word go. He committed 100% to motor racing.

CH: If he hadn't believed that in the early days do you think he would have walked away from it?

PING: He would never have got involved if he hadn't thought he could be World Champion.

DRON: I quite agree with that. He thought *if I don't get to the top in motor racing I will get to the top in something.* Had it been the church he'd probably have been well on his way to being Archbishop of Canterbury.

PING: The two other things he would have gone in to were medicine – that was the first choice – and the Army, having been at Wellington. It was an Army school and at one time he was going to go into it – but then he went to Brands for the Boxing Day meeting and his life changed.

CH: Can you just describe that moment because I've never felt it.

DRON: For me it was at the Brands Hatch motor racing stables. I wanted to do a little bit there just to see if I really did take to it. Tony Lanfranchi [motor racing character and versatile driver] took me up to the control tower and said 'you really can do this, you know.' There was nothing to do with motor racing in my family. I got taken to Goodwood a few times in the 1950s because of my aunt's interest – it was her local circuit. At the age of 12 I bought an Austin 7 for ten quid, took the body off it with an axe, marked out a circuit in the garden and started timing myself round it. I could get round in 25 seconds and no-one else could beat half a minute.

CH (to Ping): And the women get drawn in because the man has been drawn in and they go with him.

PING: Yes, that's how it was for me. I knew nothing about motor racing. Chris Ridge, a friend, was driving a Mini and he said 'come down with James' to Brands. I remember sitting in the stand at Paddock Bend and I think that would have been the first race James had ever seen. He said 'you know, this is brilliant' and it all just evolved from there.

DRON: I think the inspiring moment for me was standing at the old Nürburgring watching practice for the German Grand Prix in the 1960s and seeing Jim Clark come down the hill. It was absolute commitment. I had this idea that race drivers just sat there and steered and glided through. Clark's hands were everywhere and the gear changes were fantastic and it made the hair stand up on the back of my neck. I thought 'I've got to do this.'

The perfect setting for memories (Author).

CH: Whereas James's moment came at Paddock Hill Bend.

DRON: A friend had the same thing and he went through the motor racing stable. They put him in a Formula 3 race and he qualified on the front row. Then in the last lap of practice he went off on the outside of Paddock, bounced back right across the circuit and, up by Druids, turned over. He had three days in hospital.

CH: And that presumably ended it for him?

DRON: Technically it did, yes.

CH: James had a lot of those moments.

DRON: My second race meeting was James's first and the next one was at Snetterton. I met James there and we were quite friendly straight away. He was in the same position as me. Then we went weekend after weekend after weekend. I think we did 45 races in the year, heats and finals and everything. Looking back on it, one in ten of them were stopped at the first corner. And there were things like the lake at Oulton Park …

PING: I remember that!

DRON: The circuit was a bit slippery. The leader was a hundred yards ahead at the end of the second lap, I was third, James fifth. I went into Cascades [a left-hander] intending to get the guy in front of me and I just went wide. I had a fantastic spin at 100 miles an hour. That was my first race with seat belts and I went round so fast I didn't know where I was. I ended up on the left slightly down a bank and I saw James coming at me. I had a horrible feeling he was coming into my car but he went just over my head. He went through the advertising hoarding and I thought *that's not good.* Normally you'd have the car in first gear to set off again but I thought *no, I don't like that.* So I stopped it and got out, stumbled across to the lake. I saw bits of the front and bits of the back of his car. I saw the car upside down and Hunt in the water. I thought *right, keep your senses, take a deep breath* and just at that moment he stood up. He was 20 feet away and he'd got goggles with water behind them and bits of greenery hanging off him: Frankenstein coming out of the make-up department. He was a bit knocked about. He was wading out and I grabbed him, helped him to lie down on the ground. He wasn't making any sense because he'd had a bang on the head. He tried to tell me some dirty joke. It was a long time before the marshals got there.

PING: When he got back to the pits he didn't know whether he was coming or going. Then, Tony, you drove us home. James was not in a position to drive.

CH: Normal people might have reasoned at that stage 'I've really got to think about the rest of my life – and staying alive for that.'

DRON: Well, no. That was my point earlier. At that stage we'd been at it for six months every weekend and the risk of battle fatigue starts to set in when you think of what we had gone through *but* we had reached that point where the race at the weekend was a really big thing. Tuesday was the only day when you didn't have a pain in your stomach. On the Wednesday you started building up to the next weekend. It was the same for James, the same for everybody. We were trying absolutely as hard as we could. You were constantly looking at how you could improve your technique, how you could go quicker. James was very, very good at observing what other people did. I know he observed my driving and we talked about that. Later on in his career he observed very closely what his peers at that time were doing, Niki and Emerson, to see what he could learn from them.

CH: And, given the determined character he had, if he'd walked away, it would have beaten him.

DRON: Yes, but at that stage we were committed, we knew we could do it, we knew we were right on it and James was beginning to show that he really did have it. At the end of that season I was asked 'who do you think is this year's Formula Ford driver who could or is going to make it to the very top?' This guy was a great Tim Schenken enthusiast [an Australian, widely regarded as an outstanding F1 prospect]. I didn't believe in Schenken. I thought he was a neat product who'd been given every opportunity. I said 'James Hunt.' At the end of his Formula Ford career, by observing other people James was beginning to develop a really stunning overtaking technique. He was perfecting that last minute dive down the inside

CH: But he did throw up before the races.

DRON: All the drivers are like that! If you're not wanting to throw up before a motor race you're not trying. What frightens you is like going on stage: maybe you won't perform properly. You're not frightened of getting hurt. That really doesn't come into it at all. It's that you have *got* to put on an outstanding performance.

PING: If he made a mistake he'd say.

CH: Was he honest with himself?

DRON: In the early days, yes. I think towards the very end possibly not so much, but I think ultimately he kept a grip on what he was doing. I say that because once, late in his life, when we were doing something down at Goodwood – he'd got to the circuit in his Mercedes, one of those times when he'd got it running – he said he was thinking of going back into F1. It was something that Niki Lauda had done but looking at James at that stage I wondered whether he'd do it. I said 'is that what you really want?' Silence. That would imply that ultimately he was honest with himself. He had considered it to get out of [financial] trouble, which is the wrong reason to go back in. I think he saw that, although he had toyed with the idea.

PING: Was that when it was going to be with Williams? I talked to him at the house at Wimbledon during Wimbledon fortnight – that was when he said 'if it's raining I'll have to charge you to park your car!' – and he said he had driven a Williams, no he'd gone to test drive one and he couldn't get in. He was too big. So that was it.

CH: Which begs the question: what would James have been worth in today's currency? You hear sums like £50 million around Jenson Button and this is a bloke who's not won a race. And there was James, World Champion. What *would* he have been worth?

DRON: Yes, but he'd have screwed it up, wouldn't he!

PING: He would have done!

DRON: But it was different times.

PING: Yes, different times. You can make the comparison with any sportsman. Look at the tennis players, look at Rod Laver. They didn't get a lot, did they? Certainly in today's money the world would have been a different place for him. We would probably have missed out on having him on the BBC commentating. He wouldn't have needed to have done that.

DRON: Murray thought that James was a loose cannon who could compromise business, which he could have done. In fact James was absolutely brilliant.

PING: James couldn't have done the commentaries, Murray couldn't have done the expert analysis. James did it all in such a nice way. He didn't put Murray down, did he?

DRON: He saw how they could use each other, different as they were.

PING: I don't think anyone could match James.

DRON: He took it to a magic level and then, that last time, he got on his bike and cycled home.

PING: And he probably had no shoes on his feet either.

DRON: He turned up to someone's wedding on that bike with a suit in a holdall and changed on the pavement outside.

CH: Do you think that was partly the public schoolboy and the privileged position?

PING: No, no – that was James, that was James through and through. He was always like that. Even before the motor racing days he was always different from everyone. He did his own thing.

CH: Do you think he would have done that if he had been from a council estate in Peckham?

PING: Yes, that was him.

CH: He said outrageous things on the television because he believed them to be true. He was prepared to defend what he said and he didn't care if he upset people.

DRON: Well, he was perhaps too hard on Patrese for reasons we all know very well, but even when he

Remembering an English gentleman: Tony Dron (left), Taormina Rieck and the author (Author).

expressed outrageous opinions he knew he could defend them. He had this rather over-developed sense of right and wrong and what's fair in life. It was childlike. When he grew up and discovered what the world was really like he was tempted to say 'well, bollocks, I'll just do what I want. I know what's really right and I'll just do that as I see fit.'

PING: And did that 'because that's me.'

DRON: There was no way he would calculate to say something to boost his image. He had passionate beliefs and followed them. He said it as he saw it.

CH: He was hard on de Cesaris, and de Cesaris knew about it, but James could have said to him 'play the tape and I'll defend it.'

PING: And he could have done.

DRON: In commentating he showed his naturalness, unaffected by convention and he could think very quickly. He did *not* however think 'am I being politically correct?' I don't think he gave a stuff for television, it was just as if he was speaking to his mates.

PING: And he didn't get nervous beforehand.

DRON: It was 'so what?' He'd seen masses of celebrities so he wasn't looking up to anybody.

PING: Yes.

DRON: This is a happily trivial story. When did decimal currency come? Do you remember when you and James and my girlfriend of those days, Doro, and I were having a drink in the cellar bar of the *Wheatsheaf* at Virginia Water? James got his change and dropped one of the new 50p coins. It fell to the floor and rolled away. And he searched and searched and searched. He'd do that, wouldn't he?

PING: Yes.

DRON: He would *not* give up searching for this 50p piece. This is a point people forget: James spent most of his life effectively skint. I don't think this story is about how skint he was and how much the 50p mattered to him but it was the obsessive nature. *Here is a problem and I am not going to let it go.* And also *if I choose to buy drinks I'll buy drinks but I am not throwing money away.*

PING: And here's my story. It must have been going down to Magny-Cours just after decimalisation. Now what was the name of the guy who sponsored Gerry Birrell?

DRON: Big John.

PING: Big John had plenty of money and he paid for the drinks on the ferry and as luck would have it – completely the opposite to James – the man serving got mixed up with the new currency and gave him 50p pieces instead of 10p pieces for the change so he actually received more money than he had paid them for the drinks. That's Sod's law, isn't it? That wouldn't have happened with James. They'd have given him 10p! James struggled, from his 'collection' of old cars – he had the old Rover and the old ...

DRON: Everyone knows about the Mini.

PING: He took it to Snetterton and went to scrutineering. They said 'no, you can't race, you haven't got a passenger seat.' He put a deck chair in and went back and said 'how about this?' and they said 'oh, all right'! But, you see, that was him, he wouldn't give up. He was going to race that day and he had put everything into it to get that car ready.

DRON: There was a definite parallel between us in that we'd both been to public school, which made us fit to go into the First World War, carry a Webley [service revolver] and say *follow me chaps* over the top.

We were ideally suited for that and not much else. We had no capital behind us at all.

PING: And your parents weren't prepared to say 'here you are.'

DRON: They were not sufficiently wealthy to do that.

PING: The Hunts did nothing, they said 'down to you.'

DRON: Except they allowed James to live at home when he should have been making a career and they didn't cause a fuss when he stopped working for Telephone Rentals for 20 quid a week and tried to pursue this mad dream. I turned my back on being a chartered surveyor and James turned his back on a medical career and we decided to do this, which was a stupid, irresponsible thing to do. A medical career would ultimately have been well paid but the point I make is that, once he turned his back on this, life immediately became very difficult – even though he was in this apparently privileged position. Looking back it is a disadvantage because there were people getting into positions of power who resented anyone who spoke like that. My career did not take off until I lost my public school accent.

PING: Don't you think that the two of you really helped each other?

DRON: I think we did. That's why we travelled around together in Formula Ford – because there was a great degree of moral and real support.

PING: And everyone else was different.

DRON: We learned a lot from each other.

PING: But it was the same spirit. There was a fierce camaraderie and although you had your arguments they were all in the 'family'. And there was spirit: when I did the lap charts I didn't put the number of the car, I used to put the initials of all the drivers and James would come in afterwards and look at it. He would know exactly who was doing what.

DRON: Where would he have been today? I was thinking of him at the Goodwood Revival meeting this year and how much he would have enjoyed that.

PING: He'd have loved that. He'd have got into the old McLaren and driven it at breakneck speed.

DRON: In the old days he would drop into my house when I wasn't there and chat to my mother. There were a

Slightly off the racing line at Oulton (cartoon by Julian Kirk).

DRON
KIRK.

few lay-bys around there. I'd drive past and every now and then I'd see James with his car and his trailer having his 20-minute kip. He was physically different from other people. You shouldn't have underestimated his incredible strength – he was probably one of the strongest blokes I have ever met. He was very, very strong, wasn't he?

PING: Yes.

CH: If you look at the *Superstars*, he saw them off.

DRON: Absolutely. All these people from other sports couldn't understand that their favourite little football star and athletes in other disciplines got beaten by this racing driver. They thought racing drivers were sedentary, just driving round, they didn't understand the physical nature of it.

PING: Wasn't he the first, or one of the first, who brought the fitness aspect into the sport? He actually trained and strengthened his neck.

DRON: Before he did that first F1 meeting, the Race of Champions, he did go down to Wimbledon Football Club and trained with them to get strong. And he said 'you know, even though I did that, towards the end of that race when I was coming out of Druids I was unable to give it full throttle because, despite these neck-strengthening exercises, the acceleration down the hill meant my head was being forced back.'

PING: Friendship was important and his friends from the early days were with him right to the end.

CH: Was he a manic depressive?

PING: No. I think James was James. I wouldn't call him a manic depressive. Would you? Or do you think it was close?

DRON: I think we were probably quite similar in that respect. I don't like to draw too many parallels but I've certainly suffered from depression a bit and I think he did too.

CH: Is that because it's just you or is it motor racing?

DRON: It's nothing to do with motor racing.

PING: If you've a great talent it can affect you. Today people are only too keen to label you with something. In the good old days you were a bit down and you coped with it. At Monaco in 1970 he came off in the heats and didn't make it to the final. I can't remember exactly what happened – he probably ran into the Armco or something – and when he was unhappy he let the world know, yes he did. There was the Dave Morgan affair at Crystal Palace.

DRON: After an Oulton Park incident I felt very guilty and he said 'I dropped it same as you did.' Then there was Mallory Park a couple of weeks later. Do you remember that?

PING: Yes!

DRON: First corner and I was hard on the right-hand side going into Gerards [a long horseshoe corner]. James had his back wheels between my front and back wheels. We were close like that. I felt quite comfortable with him there but somebody else hit him, which meant that his back wheels hit the side of my car, rode over it, he hit my front left, went up in the air and I was underneath him. I'm not as stupid as I look and I hit the brakes. I locked the front right – the front left wasn't there. He went sideways in front of me, nothing I could do because I was out of control. I knocked him round and we came to rest against the side of the track. Mallory had a bank round the outside in those days, and there were the two cars neatly parked. We got out, sat on the top of the bank and we didn't say anything to each other. He took ten Embassy and a box of matches out of his pocket, passed me a cigarette, we both lit up and watched the rest of the race. Then we wandered off. We had not discussed the incident at all because there was no point. I wasn't angry with him, he wasn't angry with me – because someone else had hit him.

PING: Suzy? If he felt it was wrong you'd have thought he had the character to say to himself 'no, don't.'

DRON: Ah, but who are we to criticise? That's a very different area, that's a very tricky thing.

PING: But he was probably lonely. There he was, living in Spain as a tax exile ...

DRON: And she was physically arresting.

PING: Yes.

DRON: She had a physical presence. Extraordinary creature.

PING: Helen? James knew nothing about art but he was very proud of her and her art. Art had never crossed his life before. She gave him something to live for and that was almost the saddest thing, that he had found happiness and he knew which way he wanted to go. The madness had all gone. He was back to the old James. He went back to his budgie breeding too. I think his life was made up of parts, the early days, then the F1 days and he then went back to being the James everybody knew at the beginning. I don't think the James in the middle was really the true James.

DRON: I think he focused on being World Champion and when he'd done that he didn't really see the point of doing it over and over again. James had a great deal of interest in other things and he didn't dither with women either. You only had to go to his memorial service to see them all lined up. Amazing.

PING: Wasn't it incredible? It was in its way a wonderful occasion and I will always remember Murray could hardly get the words out. And then the party afterwards!

DRON: I went mad after that. I wandered off.

PING: You didn't go to the party?

DRON: Yes, I stayed there quite late. It was still busy when I left and I disappeared.

PING: It all came flooding back, I guess.

DRON: Yeah. So I went absent without leave for some time.

PING: One definitely felt that he was there. I don't believe in that sort of thing particularly, but he wanted his best mates to have a good time, and Suzy came back to that.

DRON: Everyone who went into Formula Ford was serious about aiming to be one thing, and that was World Champion. I recognised that James had the qualities to do it and I didn't. I won't go into why I didn't but let's say my objective was driving very well and that's what really turned me on, but James had the all-round ability, the superhuman strength, the athletic ability. He also had a great many enemies because he was such a natural person who just behaved exactly as he wanted to. That got the backs up of the authorities even then.

They went to introduce Formula Ford to Italy. Somehow the organisers got it into their heads that everyone had to have a certificate with their blood group and James had simply stated what his blood group was, so they were going to prevent him from taking part in the race. He drove his car out at the start of the race and placed it at right angles across the front of the grid. Nick Brittan and Stuart Turner [motorsport pillar and Ford executive] were standing at the back of the grandstand. Stuart Turner said 'what is his name, this person who is ruining our race?' Nick said 'James Hunt.' Stuart said 'mark my words, he is going nowhere in motorsport.' I teased Stuart with that many years later and he said 'well, you can't get them all right, can you?'

CH: Nick Brittan tells it a slightly different way but never mind!

DRON: I remember the Boxing Day meeting at Brands 1968 and afterwards we drove off to Kitzbühel to stay at the house of the parents of my girlfriend at the time. He had a horrible cold, which he recovered from very rapidly and gave to me, so I suffered from that for much of the holiday. You got him on skis, he was competitive. He had natural balance and he was outstanding in anything he did like that.

PING: He was a true natural at squash.

CH: Was he silly on the skis?

DRON: No.

CH: Was he silly off the skis?

DRON: No comment! The house had a visitors' book, a venerable thing which was breaking up, and people who had stayed made all these lovely comments over the years. Everyone signed. I was there this year [2005] and I looked to see what he'd written. It just said:

James Hunt. GREAT BRITAIN! (BRITISH)

A LIFE IN STATISTICS

THE SIGNIFICANT TRACK RACES

1967 Three races in a Mini.

1968 Formula Ford (Russell-Alexis/ Merlyn.10 races, 1 win).

1969 Formula Ford (Merlyn. 10 races, 1 win). Formula 3 (Brabham/ March. 12 races, 2 wins).

1970 Formula 3 (Lotus 59. 18 races, 2 wins).

1971 Formula 3 (March. 21 races, 4 wins). Formula 2 (March. 1 race).

1972 Formula 3 (March/ Dastle. 10 races). Formula 2 (March. 7 races).

1973 Formula 2 (Surtees. 2 races). Formula 1 (March, Surtees. 8 Grands Prix. 8th in the World Championship, 14 points).

1974 Formula 1 (March, Hesketh. 15 Grands Prix. 8th in the World Championship, 15 points).

1975 Formula 1 (Hesketh. 14 Grands Prix, 4th in the World Championship, 33 points).

1976 Formula 1 (McLaren. 16 Grands Prix, 1st World Championship, 69 points).

1977 Formula 1 (McLaren. 17 Grands Prix, 5th in the World Championship, 40 points).

1978 Formula 1 (McLaren. 16 Grands Prix. 13th in the World Championship, 8 points).

1979 Formula 1 (Wolf. 7 Grands Prix, no points and no World Championship position because you had to compete in both halves of the season).

Grands Prix: 92 races, 14 poles, 10 wins, 8 fastest laps, 179 points.

(LAT Photographic)

INDEX